中华美食系列 **3**

养生食补
Health Tonics

黄怀玲　林淑莲　著

外文出版社
Foreign Languages Press

编者的话

21世纪的现代人，身心皆处于日新月异的科技时代的巨变中。压力、紧张，甚至慢性疾病几乎威胁着每一个人。因此，"食补"、"食疗"、"药膳"等养生保健的意识逐渐受到人们的重视。

唐朝医圣孙思邈曾提出："食能排邪安脏腑，悦神爽志以资血气"。指出摄取自然食物，利用药膳调理，可以达到强健筋骨、保持身心健康之效。然而，如何在忙碌之余，烹调出营养、美味并兼有滋补作用的佳肴，是现代人的一大课题。鉴于此，本书遵循传统的烹调艺术，开发出简单易做的药膳食谱，将日常的蔬菜、水果、鱼肉与各种常见的药材一同烹调，配制出补元气、强身抗衰老的药膳美食。

本书以"吃出健康，吃出美丽"为宗旨，提供一系列美味可口的养生食谱。所谓"食籍药力，药助食威"，两者相辅相成，无论是对中、青年的强身健体、老年人的延年益寿、儿童的生长益智、女性的补血美容、男性的强精补肾等都具有实质功效。

本书文字汉英对照，喜爱中国菜的外国朋友，拥有此书，潜心习练，定会成为中国菜的烹调大师。

Editor's Note

In the 21st century we are in the era of science and technology, which are developing at an amazing speed. A healthy body is becoming ever-more important to everyone. So people have begun to show interest in taking food and medicine as tonics.

Sun Simiao, a leading Tang Dynasty doctor, once said, "Food has the function of eliminating evil influences and soothing the vital organs, cultivating one's mind and building up one's strength." He pointed out that taking natural foods or medicines can strengthen muscles and bones, and help a person keep fit. Delicious foods full of nutrition and tonic effects are also topics of interest. This book includes a list of medicated diets following traditional cooking skills using vegetables, fruits, pork and fish, together with popular herbs. The resulting dishes have the function of tonifying primordial *qi* and building up the body.

Taking "eat for health and eat for beauty" as its guideline, this book offers a series of tonic recipes. Both food and medicine supplement each other to build up health for both old and young, and especially the function of beauty treatment for women.

This book is published in bilingual format. Foreign friends who are interested in Chinese cuisine may be confident that they too can become skilled chefs in the tradition of Chinese cuisine.

烹调中所用的火候简介

1. 炸、溜、爆、炒等均用旺火，菜肴特点为嫩、脆、酥。
2. 烧、焖、煨、扣、炖等均先用大火,后用小火烹制，这种方法必须先用大火把材料烧至半熟，使材料上色后再用小火煮熟。
3. 氽、涮、熬、蒸等烹调方法所采用的火力，应根据材料而定，一般质嫩易碎者宜用小火，质老而又体大者则用大火。
4. 煎、贴均以少量油作为传热方法，其菜肴特点为外香酥、里软嫩，具有浓厚的油香味，宜用温火。
5. 注意掌握油温，材料过油是菜肴在烹调前一项重要的准备工作，也是制作过程中常用的方法，一道菜品质的好、坏与过油关系非常大，加热时间掌握不好，那么菜品质就达不到标准。

芡汁的种类和用途

芡汁是指烹调过程中所加入的液体调味品和淀粉的总称。

芡汁按其稠度分为浓芡、薄芡两类，若按调制方法又可分为碗芡（对调味汁芡）、跑马芡（任芡）两种。

    1. 碗芡

    即各种调味料和水淀粉同放一个碗内溶合，适于用旺火爆、炒、溜各种菜肴。

    2. 跑马芡

    即水淀粉,适用于烧、烩、扒、扣等烹调方法,菜肴起锅前加入。

刀工的基本常规

一、基本要求:

1. 厨师所用菜墩要干净整洁，刀口要锋利，必备一条洁净的抹布，工作时要求干净利落。
2. 精神要集中、专心一致，操刀时要运用自如，落刀时要稳、准、狠、匀。
3. 必须根据材料的特点来决定相应的加工方法，然后用刀将材料切成整齐划一、清爽利落并符合烹调要求的形状。
4. 要根据材料的性质采用不同刀法（例如牛、羊肉要横切，鸡肉要顺切）。
5. 合理使用材料，以便物尽其用，减少损耗。

二、用刀的规矩:

1. 厨师要牢记刀和墩是不分离的，也就是说，厨师不能持刀到别处去，用后必须摆放在固定的容器内。
2. 刀若暂时不用，要将刀刃朝外前方放在墩子中央，刀把刀刃不能超出墩子边沿，以免伤到人。
3. 杜绝持刀玩耍，以防误伤。
4. 爱护刀墩，刀用后宜刷洗擦干，以防生锈，若长期不用，一定要擦油保存。

烹调中用火的经验

火候是烹调菜肴的关键，对于菜肴质量起着决定性作用，也是衡量厨师技术水平的重要标准。

烹调不同的菜肴需运用不同的火候，这是每位厨师必须掌握的，但有一个普遍的规律，即材料加热时间短则嫩，时间长则透、时间久则烂。如何做到嫩而不生、透而不老、烂而不化，那就要看厨师的水平了。

厨师掌握火候的关键在于观察火力，充分了解材料性质和受热的变化，以及所加工材料的质地，刀口粗细等等。

Introduction for Degree of Heating

1. Fry, saute and add thick sauce, fry briefly, stir fry: Cook by high heat to make the dish tender and crisp.
2. Roast, stew, simmer: Cook by high heat first till half done, then colour the dishes, turn to simmer later on till well done.
3. Evaporate, boil, steam: It depends on the ingredients. If it's tender and fragile, cook by simmer, if it's hard and big, cook by high heat then.
4. Decoct: Cook by temperate with less oil to make the inside of the dish tender, and the surface will be crisp.
5. Be care of the degree of heating: It's the most important step before cooking. Also it can decide whether the dish is going to be successful or fail.

How to Make and How to Use the Thick Sauce

It's made by cassava starch with water. Usually combine it with dish to thicken the taste of the dish. We can divide the thick sauce into two different kinds by the way how it was made.

1. Bowl thick sauce: Mix all the condiments with cassava starch and water in a bowl, pour them into the dish, fry by high heat.
2. Temporary thick sauce: Mix all the condiments with cassava starch and water first, dressing it on the top of the dish when it is ready to serve.

The Basic Rules of Using Knife

A. Basic Requirements:
1. The chopping board has to be very clean, the knife has to be sharp, it is necessary to prepare a nice clean towel too.
2. Be absolutely concentrate on your work. When you use the knife, stable, on mark, nice shape are things you need to be careful.
3. Cook each single ingredient by its own character, cut it into the right shape which fits the dish's style.
4. Cut the ingredient by its natural line.
5. Use everything useable, do not waste.

B. Basic Rules:
1. Remember, knife and chopping board can not be apart. Don't take the knife to go anywhere far from the chopping board —— where it should be. After using the knife, put it in a exact safty place.
2. When the knife is not in use, leave it in the centre of the chopping board to avoid accidents.
3. Never play the knife to avoid any accidentally injure.
4. Cherish and do good protecting to your chopping board. If you are not using it for a long term, make sure that it's very clean and has been settled in a nice place.

Experience of Heating

It is the most important key for cooking. It can decide whether the dish is going to be successful or fail, it also can tell how the cook has done.

Cook different dish by different heat. Cook for just a short time, the dish will be tender. cook for a long time, the dish will be well-done. How to cook a famous dish tender but not rare, not tough, and not over-done, it depends on the cook's skill. A good cook will see the heat, knowing what will happen when a single ingredient meets the heat, knowing each ingredient's character and the way of cutting.

目 录　CONTENTS

十全大补乌骨鸡
Stew Dark-Skinned Hen with Herbs

【材料】
①母乌骨鸡1只。
②白术、熟地、白芍各20克，党参、茯苓、当归、黄芪各15克，炙甘草、川芎各10克，肉桂5克。
③红枣10粒，枸杞10克。

【作法】
❶ 乌骨鸡洗净，去油脂，剁块，氽烫去血水。药材用水冲洗干净，沥干水份备用。红枣泡软。
❷ 取一炖锅，将鸡块、药材放入，加水盖过材料，大火煮开后，转小火炖煮约1小时即可。

【Ingredients】
① 1 dark-skinned hen ② 20g. each of atractylodes (Bai Zhu), root of Chinese foxglove (Shu Di Huang), white paeonia (Bai Shao); 15g. each of codonopsis pilosula (Dang Shen), tuckahoe, angelica and astranglus membranaceus (Huang Qi); 10g. each of licorice root and the rhizome of ChuanXiong; 5g. cinnamon ③ 10 red dates; 10g. fruit of Chinese wolfberry.

【Methods】
❶Rinse hen, cut into small pieces, and then blanch in the boiling water. Rinse all the herbage and drain. Soak red dates until soft.
❷Put hen, herbage in a pot, then add in the water which covers the herbage and then cook with high heat. After boiling, turn to low heat to stew for about. 1 hour.

【功效】
可改善面色苍白，食欲不振、气血两虚、四肢无力、头晕目眩等。
【Efficiency】
Imporve the debility of body, dizzy of head, dim eyes.

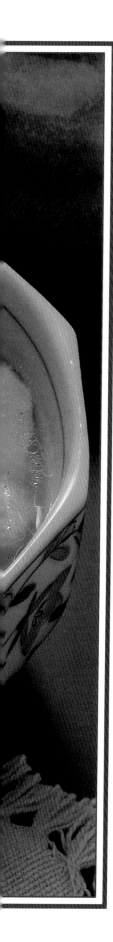

鲍鱼萝卜肉片汤
Abalone Soup with Radish and Lean

【材料】
① 小里脊肉 150 克。
② 鲍鱼 1 只。
③ 萝卜 1 根、葱 1 根。

【调味料】
(A)料：盐、香油各适量。

【作法】
❶ 小里脊肉洗净、切片。鲍鱼切片，汤汁留用。萝卜去皮切厚片、葱切段。
❷ 炖锅内加适量水、鲍鱼汤汁、肉片、萝卜和鲍鱼，大火煮开后，加入葱段，改小火煮约 30 分钟，加(A)料调味即可。

【Ingredients】
① 150g. lean ② 1 abalone ③ 1 radish; 1 scallion.

【Seasoning】
(A)proper salt and sesame oil

【Methods】
❶Rinse and slice lean; slice abalone; pare and cut radish into thick slices. Cut scallion into small sections.
❷Put proper water, radish, abalone soup, sliced lean and abalone in a pot to cook with high heat; after boiling, put scallion in and turn to low heat to cook for 30 mins. Add seasoning (A) in.

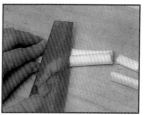

【功效】
滋阴清热，益精明目，开胃助消化。
【Efficiency】
Relieve heat. Help digestion. Good for eyes and stomach.

小米糕

【材料】
黑糯米·················250 克
樱桃·····················1 罐
【调味料】
黄砂糖 1 碗。
【作法】
❶ 黑糯米洗净泡水后蒸熟。
❷ 熟糯米加黄砂糖拌匀后，
倒入铝箔杯中即可。

Glutinous Rice Cake

【Ingredients】
250g. black glutinous rice, 1
jar of cherry.
【Seasoning】
1 bowl of granulated sugar.
【Methods】
❶Clean glutinous rice, soak
in water and steam.
❷Stir the black glutinous rice
with sugar, put on the tinfoil cup.

杏仁豆腐

【材料】
杏仁豆腐·················1 块
季节水果·················适量
（亦可用水果罐头代替）
【调味料】
糖适量。
【作法】
❶ 糖水煮沸后放入冰箱冰
镇。
❷ 杏仁豆腐、季节水果均切
小块。
❸ 食用前，将杏仁豆腐、季
节水果倒入冰糖水中即
可。

Almond Dou-Fu

【Ingredients】
1 piece of almond Dou-Fu, sea-
son fruit (canned fruit)
【Seasoning】
sugar.
【Methods】
❶Boiling the sugar and water,
cool down in refrigerator.
❷Cube the almond Dou-Fu
and fruit.
❸Put the almond Dou-Fu, fruit
in the cold sugar water before serving.

黄豆芽鲤鱼汤
Carp Soup with Bean Sprouts

【材料】
①鲤鱼1条。
②通草10克、黄豆芽100克。

【调味料】
(A) 料：米酒1大匙、盐、香油适量。

【作法】
❶ 鲤鱼去内脏、洗净。黄豆芽洗净。
❷ 锅内放水，黄豆芽、通草煮开后，转小火煮约30分钟，再将鲤鱼放入，煮至鱼熟，拣去通草，加(A)料调味即可。

【Ingredients】
① 1 carp ② 10g. tetrapanax papyriferus (Tong Cao); 100g. bean sprout

【Seasoning】
(A) 1 tbsp. rice wine; proper salt and sesame oil

【Methods】
❶ Remove the viscera of carp and rinse. Rinse bean sprouts.
❷ Cook bean sprouts, Tong-Cao with water; after boiling, turn to low heat to cook for 30 mins, then put carp in to continue cooking until the carp is done. Remove Tong-Cao and add seasoning (A) in.

【功效】
利水通乳，可治乳汁不足。

【Efficiency】
Help breast development.

- -

蛤蜊萝卜丝汤
Clams Soup with Carrot

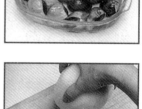

【材料】
①蛤蜊250克。
②萝卜1个、葱1根。
③高汤6杯。

【调味料】
(A) 料：酒1茶匙、盐、胡椒粉、香油各适量。

【作法】
❶ 蛤蜊加盐吐沙后，洗净。萝卜去皮、刨丝。葱洗净、切末。
❷ 锅内放入高汤、萝卜丝，煮开，转小火煮至萝卜丝呈透明时加入蛤蜊，转大火煮至蛤蜊开口，加(A)料调味后撒上葱末即可。

【Ingredients】
① 250g. clams ② 1 radish; 1 scallion
③ 6 cups of broth

【Seasoning】
(A) 1 tbsp. wine, proper salt, pepper powder and spice oil.

【Methods】
❶ Soak clams in salty water and then rinse. Pare and shred radish. Rinse and mince scallion.
❷ Cook shredded radish with broth; after boiling, turn to low heat to cook; put clams when radish becomes transparent and then turn to high heat to continue cooking until clams open. Add seasoning (A) in and sprinkle minced scallion.

【功效】
消暑、解渴、助消化。

【Efficiency】
Relieve heat. Help digestion.

八珍鸡汤
Ba-Zhen Chicken Soup

【材料】
①鸡半只。
②当归、川芎、熟地、炒白芍、炙甘草、白术、茯苓、党参各15克。红枣10粒、枸杞5克。

【调味料】
(A)料：米酒2大匙、盐适量。

【作法】
❶ 鸡去杂质、洗净、剁块，余烫去血水。药材快速冲洗后沥干水份。
❷ 备一炖锅，放入鸡块，药材、红枣、米酒及水，煮开后改小火炖煮至肉烂，加盐调味即可。

【Ingredients】
① ½ frec range chicken ② 15g. each of angelica, rhizome of Chuan Xiong; root of Chinese foxglove (Shu Di Huang); white paeonia root (Bai Shao); licorice root. atractylodes (Bai Zhu); tuckahoe; codonopsis pilosula (Dang Shen); 10 red dates; 5g. fruit of Chinese wolfberry.

【Seasoning】
(A) 2 tbsp. rice wine; proper salt.

【Methods】
❶Rinse chicken, cut into pieces and blanch in boiling water. Rinse all the herbage, and then drain. Soak red dates until soft.
❷Put chicken, herbage, red dates, rice wine and water in pot to cook with high heat. After boiling, turn to low heat to stew until chicken is done and soft. Add salt in.

【功效】
养血补气，活血化瘀，增进产妇体力及乳汁。
【Efficiency】
Make blood; nourish vitality; strengthen the body; increase milk for women after childbirth.

什锦炒饭

【材料】
冷饭⋯⋯⋯⋯⋯⋯⋯1大碗
素火腿⋯⋯⋯⋯⋯⋯1小块
香菇⋯⋯⋯⋯⋯⋯⋯2朵
冷冻青豆仁、玉米粒、
胡萝卜⋯⋯⋯⋯⋯各¼杯

【调味料】
低钠盐1小匙、胡椒少许、酱油1小匙。

【作法】
❶ 香菇泡软去蒂，素火腿切丁。
❷ 起油锅，先爆香香菇、素火腿，再加冷冻蔬菜拌炒，加调味料拌匀后盛起。
❸ 另起油锅，将冷饭倒入炒热，加少许盐、酱油调味，再倒 ❷ 材料同炒即可。

Fry Rice

【Ingredients】
1 big bowl of rice, 1 cube of vegetarian ham, 2 black mushrooms, ¼ cup of frozen green peas, ¼ cup of corn, ¼ cup of carrot.

【Seasoning】
1 tbsp. of low sodium salt, 1 tbsp. of soy sauce, pepper.

【Methods】
❶Cut the stems of the black mushrooms off and soak, dice the vegetarian ham.
❷Heat oil, sante black mushroom, vegetarian ham, add frozen vegetable to fry, stir with spicies.
❸Heat another oil, fry the rice, add salt, soy sauce, put ❷ingredients inside.

什锦炒面

【材料】
过油面⋯⋯⋯⋯⋯⋯250克
香菇⋯⋯⋯⋯⋯⋯⋯2朵
金针菇⋯⋯⋯⋯⋯⋯1小把
胡萝卜⋯⋯⋯⋯⋯⋯1小块
油菜、榨菜丝⋯⋯⋯⋯少许

【调味料】
低钠盐1小匙、酱油1大匙、蚝油1大匙、糖少许、香油少许。

【作法】
❶ 香菇泡软去蒂切丝，榨菜丝泡水去咸味，金针菇氽烫，胡萝卜切长条。
❷ 起油锅，先倒入香菇爆香，再加金针菇、榨菜、胡萝卜炒熟，加水、调味料煮开，再放过油面入锅拌炒至汤汁收干。
❸ 起锅前放油菜快炒即可。

Fry Noddles

【Ingredients】
250g. oiled noddle, 2 black mushroom, 1 banch of golden mushroom, salted mustard green shredded, 1 slice of carrot, rape.

【Seasoning】
1 tbsp. of low sodium salt, 1 tbsp. of soy sauce, 1 tbsp. of vegetarian oyster sauce, a pinch of sugar, and white sesame oil.

【Methods】
❶Cut the stems of black mushrooms off, soak and shredd. rinse salted mustard green. Blanch the golden mushroom, cut the carrot by strings.
❷ Heat oil, sante the black mushrooms, add golden

mushrooms, salted mustard green, carrot to fry, add water, spicies, put the oiled noddle until the soup is thick.
❸Add rape and stir quickly before turn off.

21

沙参玉竹炖猪心

Stew Pig's Heart with Sha Shen and Yu Zhu

【材料】
①猪心 1 个。
②沙参、玉竹各 20 克、红枣 8 粒。

【调味料】
(A) 料：盐适量。

【作法】
❶ 猪心挤出血水、洗净，余烫备用。药材快速冲洗，红枣泡软。
❷ 炖锅内加水，将全部材料放入，煮开后改小火炖煮约 1 小时，加盐调味即可。

【Ingredients】
① 1 pig's heart ② 20g. each of root of beech silvertop (Sha Shen) and solomonseal rhizome (Yu Zhu); 8 red dates.

【Seasoning】
(A) Proper salt.

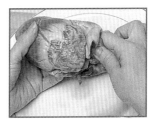

【Methods】
❶Clean and rinse pig's heart; blanch in boiling water. Rinse herbage; soak red dates.
❷Put water and all the ingredients in pot to cook. After boiling, turn to low heat to stew for 1 hour. Add salt in.

【功效】
润肺止咳、养胃生津。
【Efficiency】
Moisten lung and stop coughing. Good for stomach.

杜仲炖猪尾
Stew Pig's Tail with Du Zhong

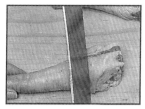

【材料】
①猪尾1条。
②川断25克、杜仲30克。

【调味料】
(A)料：盐适量。

【作法】
❶ 猪尾洗净，剁块，余烫去血水。药材快速冲洗，沥干备用。
❷ 炖锅内加水，加入猪尾与药材，煮开后改小火炖煮至肉烂，加(A)料调味即可。

【Ingredients】
① 1 pig's tail ② 25g. teasel; 30g. eucommia bark (Du Zhong)

【Seasoning】
(A) proper salt

【Methods】
❶Rinse and cut pig's tail into pieces; blanch in boiling water. Rinse herbage and drain.
❷Put water, pig's tail and herbage in pot to cook; after boiling, turn to low heat to stew until pig's tail is soft. Add seasoning (A) in.

【功效】
补肝肾，强健筋骨，可治腰膝劳损、疼痛。

【Efficiency】
Good for liver and kidney. Cure backache.

杜仲腰花汤
Pig's kidney Soup with Du Zhong

【材料】
①腰子1副。
②杜仲20克、枸杞10克、老姜1块。

【调味料】
(A)料：酒2大匙、盐适量。

【作法】
❶ 腰子对剖、去白筋，斜切花纹，漂洗干净后余烫去腥。药材稍冲洗、沥干。老姜切片。
❷ 将材料②加水5杯，煮开后改小火熬约1小时，开大火，加入腰子与(A)料，再煮开即可关火。

【Ingredients】
① 1 pair of pig's kidney ② 20g. eucommia bark (Du Zhong); 10g. fruit of Chinese wolfberry; 1 ginger

【Seasoning】
(A) 2 tbsp. wine; proper salt

【Methods】
❶Cut kidney into halves; remove the membrane; score in a crisscross pattern and soak in water. Rinse kidney and then blanch in boiling water. Rinse herbage and drain. Slice ginger.
❷Stew ingredient ② in 5 cups of water and then turn to low heat to stew for 1 hour after boiling; turn to high heat while putting kidney and seasoning (A) in to cook until boiling again.

【功效】
补肝益肾，强壮筋骨。

【Efficiency】
Good for liver and kidney. Strengthen the body.

咖哩炒饭

【材料】
冷饭·····················1 大碗
冷冻蔬菜·················适量
素火腿·····················1 块
【调味料】
低钠盐 2 小匙、咖哩粉适量。
【作法】
❶ 素火腿切丁。
❷ 起油锅，爆香火腿再倒入冷冻蔬菜炒软，加咖哩粉拌炒后盛起。
❸ 另起油锅，倒入冷饭入锅炒匀，加少许盐和❷料拌炒后即可盛盘。

Fry Curry Rice

【Ingredients】
1 bowl of rice, frozen vegetables, 1 cube of vegetarian ham.
【Seasoning】
2 tbsp. of low sodium salt, curry powder.
【Methods】
❶Dice the vegetarian ham.
❷Heat oil, sante the vegetarian ham, fry frozen vegetables till soft, add curry powder.
❸Heat another oil, add rice, salt and the ingredients❷to fry.

雪菜年糕

【材料】
浙江年糕·················2 条
雪里红···················2 棵
香菇·····················2 朵
红辣椒···················1 根
【调味料】
低钠盐 2 小匙、香油少许、酱油 1 小匙、糖½ 小匙、水少许。
【作法】
❶ 年糕切斜片，香菇切丝，雪里红、红辣椒均切细丁。
❷ 起油锅，爆香红辣椒、香菇丝，年糕入锅加少许水煮软，再放雪里红、及调味料拌炒，盛盘。

New Year Cake with Potherb Mustard

【Ingredients】
2 strip of Zhejiang's cake, 2 potherb mustard, 2 black mushroom, 1 chilli.
【Seasoning】
2 tbsp. of low sodium salt, a pinch of white sesame oil, 1 tbsp. of soy sauce, ½ tbsp. of sugar, water.
【Methods】
❶Slice the new year cake, shred the black mushroom, cube the potherb mustard and chilli.
❷Heat oil, sante chilli, black mushroom shredded, fry the new year cake to be soft, add potherb mustard, spicies.

人参乌骨鸡
Stew Dark-Skinned Hen with Ginsengs

【材料】
① 母乌骨鸡1只。
② 参须6～7条、枸杞10克、红枣10粒。
③ 米酒2大匙。

【作法】
❶ 乌骨鸡洗净，去油脂，剁块，汆烫去血水。药材快速冲洗后沥干水份。红枣泡软备用。
❷ 取一炖锅，放入鸡块与药材，加水与米酒，大火煮开后，转小火煮约1小时即可。

【Ingredients】
① 1 dark-skinned hen ② 6～7 pcs. of ginsengs; 10g. fruit of Chinese wolfberry; 10g. red dates ③ 2 tbsp. rice wine.

【Methods】
❶ Rinse hen, cut into pieces and then blanch in boiling water. Rinse herbage, then drain. Soak red dates until soft.
❷ Put hen, all herbage, water and rice wine in pot to cook with high heat; after boiling, turn to low heat to continue cooking for about. 1 hour.

【功效】
体虚、贫血、手脚冰冷者，具补充元气之效。
【Efficiency】
Nourish vitality for a weak, and anemic people.

羊肉炉
Stew Mutton with Herbs

【材料】
①带皮羊肉750克。
②川芎、黄芪、陈皮、肉桂、桂枝各10克、当归3片、甘草1片、枸杞15克、红枣10粒、老姜1块。

【调味料】
(A)料：米酒2～3瓶、黑芝麻油3大匙。

【作法】
❶ 羊肉洗净，切块，氽烫去血水、药材快速冲洗干净，沥干备用。红枣泡软、老姜切片。

❷ 锅烧热，下黑芝麻油爆香姜片，再倒入羊肉翻炒后盛起放入炖锅中，加酒炖煮至肉烂即可。

【Ingredients】
① 750g. mutton ② 10g. each of rhizome of Chuan Xiong, astranglus membranaceus (Huang Qi) tangerine peel, cinnamon bark, ramulus cinnamomi (Gui Zhi); 3 slices of angelica; 1 Slice of licorice root; 15g. fruit of Chinese wolfberry; 10 red dates; 1 ginger

【Seasonings】
(A) 2～3 bottles of rice wine; 3 tbsp. black sesame oil

【Methods】
❶Rinse and cut mutton into small pieces. Blanch them in boiling water. Rinse herbage; drain. Soak red dates. Slice ginger.
❷Heat the pot, fry ginger with black sesame oil until fragrant and put mutton in to stir-fry; then remove to a pot for stewing with rice wine until mutton is soft and done.

【功效】
可促进血液循环，增温御寒。
【Efficiency】
Promote blood circulation and keep out cold.

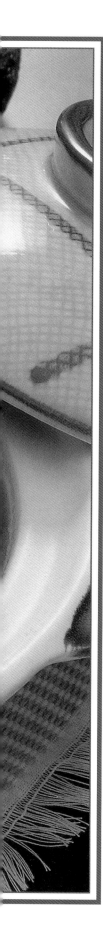

宫保鲜鱿

【材料】
素鱿鱼·······························200克
去皮花生米··························100克
青椒·································1个
干辣椒································6根
姜··································1小块

【调味料】
低钠盐1小匙、酱油2大匙、糖1小匙、酒1小匙、香油1小匙。

【作法】
❶ 素鱿鱼川烫备用。青椒去籽切片，姜去皮切片。
❷ 起油锅，放入干辣椒和姜片爆香，再将素鱿鱼和青椒片入锅略炒。
❸ 调味料调匀后倒入 ❷ 的锅中拌炒，入味后撒上花生米即可起锅。

Spicy Vegetarian Squid

【Ingredients】
200g. vegetarian squid, 100g. peanut (strip off), 1 green bell pepper, 6 dry chilli, 1 cube of ginger.

【Seasoning】
1 tbsp. of low sodium salt, 2 tbsp. of soy sauce, 1 tbsp. of sugar, 1 tbsp. of wine, 1 tbsp. of white sesame oil.

【Methods】
❶Blanch the vegetarian squid, keep the seeds of green bell pepper away and slice, strip ginger and slice.
❷Heat oil, sante dry chilli and ginger, add vegetarian squid and sliced green bell pepper.
❸Mix the spicies. Put it in ingredients❷to fry, then spread peanut before turn off.

牛蒡莲藕排骨汤
Stew Spareribs with Burdock and Lotus Root

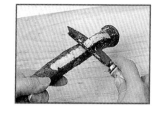

【材料】
① 排骨 600 克。
② 牛蒡 250 克、莲藕 3～4 节。
【调味料】
(A) 料：盐适量。
【作法】
❶ 排骨洗净，氽汤去血水。牛蒡、莲藕去外皮，切片，浸泡盐水。
❷ 锅内加水煮开，放入排骨、牛蒡、莲藕，煮至排骨、莲藕松软加(A) 料调味即可。

【Ingredients】
① 600g. sparerib ② 250g. burdock fruit; 3～4 nodes of lotus root.
【Seasoning】
(A) proper salt.
【Methods】
❶ Rinse and blanch spareribs in boiling water. Pare and slice burdock fruit and lotus root and then soak them in salty water.
❷ Put spareribs, burdock, lotus root in the boiling water to stew until spareribs and lotus root are soft. Add seasoning (A) in.

【功效】
润肠通便，健胃益气。
【Efficiency】
Moisten digestive apparatus. Nourish vitality. Good for stomoch.

山药炖排骨
Stew Spareribs with Yam

【材料】
① 排骨 500 克。
② 新鲜山药 600 克，枸杞 10 克。
【调味料】
(A) 料：盐适量。
【作法】
❶ 排骨洗净，氽烫去血水。山药去皮、切块。
❷ 锅内加水，煮开，放入全部材料，煮至排骨、山药软烂，加盐调味即可。

【Ingredients】
① 500g. spareribs ② 600g. fresh yam; 10g. fruit of Chinese wolfberry.
【Seasoning】
(A) proper salt
【Methods】
❶ Rinse and blanch spareribs in boiling water. Pare and cube yam.
❷ Put all the ingredients in the boiling water to cook until spareribs and yam are soft. Add salt in.

【功效】
养肝明目、增强体力。
【Efficiency】
Good for liver and eyes. Increase energy.

冬虫夏草炖鸡汤
Stew Chicken Soup with Dongchong-Xiacao

【材料】
①鸡半只。
②冬虫夏草15枝、枸杞5克。
③葱1根、姜1块。
④酒2大匙、盐适量。

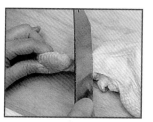

【作法】
❶ 鸡洗净，去油脂，剁块，氽烫去血水。冬虫夏草洗净，泡水约1小时。葱切长段，姜切片。
❷ 取一炖锅，放入鸡块、药材、葱段与姜片，加入米酒、水，大火煮开后，用小火炖煮约2小时即可。（可视个人口味酌量加盐。）

【Ingredients】
① ½ free range chicken ② 15 pcs. of Chinese caterpillar fungus (Dongchong-Xiacao); 5g. fruit of Chinese wolfberry. ③ 1 scallion; 1 ginger ④ 2 tbsp. wine, proper salt.

【Methods】
❶Rinse chicken, cut into pieces and then blanch in boiling water. Rinse berbage and soak them in water for about 1 hour. Cut scallion into sections. Slice ginger.
❷Put chicken, herbage, scallion, ginger, rice wine, and water in pot and then cook with high heat. After boiling, turn to low heat to cook for 2 hours. (Adding salt depends on one's favor)

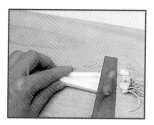

【功效】
补精益气，可治阳痿、遗精、腰酸背痛。
【Efficiency】
Nourish vitality; cure impotence, nocturnal emission and backache.

八宝辣酱面

【材料】

过油面···250 克
口蘑··2 个
豆腐干···2 片
素火腿··1 小块
胡萝卜··1 小块
玉米粒··少许
荸荠··2 个
青椒···¼ 个
红辣椒··1 根

【调味料】

低钠盐 2 小匙、辣豆瓣酱 2 大匙、糖 ½ 小匙、水少
许。

【作法】

❶ 口蘑切片，豆腐干、素火腿、胡萝卜、荸荠、青
　椒均切丁，红辣椒切末。

❷ 起油锅，爆香红辣椒后，倒入玉米粒加 ❶ 其他
　的材料同炒。

❸ 将过油面和少许水入 ❷ 的锅中加上调味料拌匀，
　炒至汤汁收干，即可盛盘。

Spicy Noddles with Eight Ingredients

【Ingredients】

250g. of oiled noddles, 2 mushrooms, 2 pieces of dry bean curd, 1 cube of vegetarian ham, 1 cube of carrot, corn, 2 water chestnut,¼ green bell pepper, 1 chilli.

【Seasoning】

2 tbsp. of low sodium salt, 2 tbsp. of spicy bean sauce, ½ tbsp. of sugar, water.

【Methods】

❶Slice mushrooms, dice dry bean curd, vegetarian ham, carrot, water chestnuts, green bell pepper. Chop the chilli.

❷Heat oil, sante chilli, add corn and❶ingredients to fry.

❸Add oiled noddles and water in❷and stir with spicies, fry till the soup is thicken.

八宝辣酱面

【材料】

过油面·······················250克
口蘑····························2个
豆腐干···························2片
素火腿·························1小块
胡萝卜·························1小块
玉米粒···························少许
荸荠····························2个
青椒···························¼个
红辣椒··························1根

【调味料】

低钠盐2小匙、辣豆瓣酱2大匙、糖½小匙、水少许。

【作法】

❶ 口蘑切片，豆腐干、素火腿、胡萝卜、荸荠、青椒均切丁，红辣椒切末。

❷ 起油锅，爆香红辣椒后，倒入玉米粒加 ❶ 其他的材料同炒。

❸ 将过油面和少许水入 ❷ 的锅中加上调味料拌匀，炒至汤汁收干，即可盛盘。

Spicy Noddles with Eight Ingredients

【Ingredients】

250g. of oiled noddles, 2 mushrooms, 2 pieces of dry bean curd, 1 cube of vegetarian ham, 1 cube of carrot, corn, 2 water chestnut, ¼ green bell pepper, 1 chilli.

【Seasoning】

2 tbsp. of low sodium salt, 2 tbsp. of spicy bean sauce, ½ tbsp. of sugar, water.

【Methods】

❶ Slice mushrooms, dice dry bean curd, vegetarian ham, carrot, water chestnuts, green bell pepper. Chop the chilli.

❷ Heat oil, sante chilli, add corn and ❶ ingredients to fry.

❸ Add oiled noddles and water in ❷ and stir with spicies, fry till the soup is thicken.

麻油腰花
Cook Pig's Kidney with Sesame oil

【材料】
①腰子 1 副。
②老姜 1 块。
【调味料】
(A) 料：米酒 2 杯、黑芝麻油 3 大匙。
【作法】
❶ 腰子对剖，剔除白筋，漂洗干净后汆烫去腥。
❷ 腰子斜切花纹，老姜拍碎。
❸ 炒锅烧热，放入黑芝麻油，爆香老姜后，加酒煮开，放
　 入腰花再煮开即可。

【Ingredients】
① 1 pair of pig's kidney ② 1 old ginger.
【Seasoning】
(A) 2 cups of rice wine; 3 tbsp. black sesame oil
【Methods】
❶ Cut kidney into halves; remove the membrane and then
　 blanch in boiling water after rinsing.
❷ Score kidney in a crisscross pattern, chop ginger.
❸ Heat the pot, pour black sesame oil, then fry ginger until
　 fragrant; add rice wine in to cook umtil boiling, then put
　 kidney in to cook until boiling.

【功效】
补肾壮阳，固精。
【Efficiency】
Good for Kidney. Nourish vitality.

桑枝炖母鸡
Stew Hen with Sang Zhi

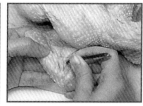

【材料】
① 母鸡1只。
② 桑枝75克、枸杞10克。

【调味料】
(A) 料：盐适量

【作法】
❶ 母鸡洗净，余烫去血水。药材稍冲洗。
❷ 炖锅内加水，放入药材与鸡，大火煮开后，转小火煮至肉烂，加(A)料调味即可。

【Ingredients】
① 1 hen ② 75g. morus alba L. (Sang Zhi); 10g. fruit of Chinese wolfberry.

【Seasoning】
(A) proper salt

【Methods】
❶ Rinse and blanch hen in boiling water. Rinse herbage.
❷ Cook herbage, hen with water; after boiling, turn to low heat to cook until hen is soft. Add seasoning (A) in.

【功效】
补精益髓，祛风除湿。
【Efficiency】
Nourish vitality. Cure rheumatism.

陈皮萝卜瘦身汤
Radish Soup with Tangerine Peel

【材料】
① 萝卜1根。
② 陈皮5克、山楂10克。
③ 香菜1棵。

【调味料】
(A) 料：盐适量。

【作法】
❶ 萝卜去皮，切滚刀块，药材稍冲洗。香菜洗净，切末。
❷ 锅内加水，放入萝卜、药材，大火煮开后，改小火煮至萝卜熟烂，加(A)料调味，再撒上香菜末即可。

【Ingredients】
① 1 radish ② 5g. tangerine peel (Chen Pi); 10g. Chinese hawthorn (Shan Zha)
③ 1 coriander

【Seasoning】
(A) proper salt

【Methods】
❶ Pare and cube radish. Rinse herbage. Rinse and mince coriander.
❷ Cook radish and herbage with water, after boiling, turn to low heat to continue cooking until radish is soft. Add seasoning (A) in and sprinkle minced coriander.

【功效】
化痰止咳，助消化。可预防便秘、脂肪堆积。
【Efficiency】
Prevent phlegm from forming; stop coughing and help digestion. Avoid constipation and fat accumulation.

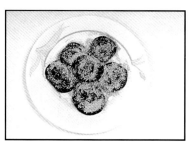

粉蒸鲜菇

【材料】
鲜香菇……………………10 朵
苜蓿芽…………………… 适 量
蒸肉粉…………………… 1 碗
香菜…………………… 少许

【调味料】
低钠盐 1 小匙、酱油 1 大匙、糖 1 小匙、香油少许。

【作法】
❶ 鲜香菇去蒂斜切成半，入油锅炸熟，捞出沥油。

❷ 在大碗内倒入蒸肉粉和炸过的香菇。起油锅，将调味料煮开后，倒入大碗中拌匀。

❸ 将沾好蒸肉粉的香菇放入蒸碗（碗中先抹上色拉油）中，在蒸锅里以大火蒸 15 分钟。盘中以苜蓿芽垫底，把蒸好的香菇倒扣于其上，缀以香菜。

Steam Black Mushroom

【Ingredients】
10 black mushrooms. 1 bowl of steam flour, clover sprouts, parsley.

【Seasoning】
1 tbsp. of low sodium salt, 1 tbsp. of soy sauce, 1 tbsp. of sugar, white sesame oil.

【Methods】
❶Cut the stem of black mushroom off, cut them into halves, fry and drain.

❷Put the steam flour and fried black mushroom in a big bowl. Heat oil, fry the spicies, stir them in the bowl.

❸Put the black mushrooms in the steam bowl (paint oil on the bowl). Steam for 15 mins. by large fire. Put the clover sprouts on the dish, then put the black mushroom, garnish with parsley.

桂花糖藕

【材料】
莲藕…………………… 1 条
糯米…………………… 1 小碗

【调味料】
冰糖 150 克、桂花酱少许。

【作法】
❶ 莲藕去尾洗净，糯米洗净沥干水分。

❷ 莲藕里的洞以糯米填满，并以擀面杖把洞口敲平，入沸水煮 1 个小时，捞出。

❸ 将煮好的莲藕皮削掉，切厚片置于碗中，加冰糖和桂花酱入蒸笼蒸 1 小时，待凉后放进冰箱里冰镇即可。

Sweet Osmanthus Lotus Roots

【Ingredients】
1 strip of lotus roots, 1 bowl of glutinous rice.

【Seasoning】
150g. rock candy, a little bit of sweet osmanthus sauce.

【Methods】
❶Clean and cut the bottom of lotus roots. Clean the glutinous rice and strain.

❷Put the glutinous rice inside the holes of the lotus roots, knock the hole by a stick, cook in boiling water for 1 hour.

❸ Strip the lotus roots, slice thickly, put in the bowl, add rock candy and sweet osmanthus, steam for 1 hour, then put in the refrigerator.

黄豆炖猪蹄
Stew Pig's Foot with Soybean

【材料】
① 猪蹄 1 只。
② 黄豆 200 克、金针菜 50 克。

【调味料】
(A) 料：盐适量、酒 2 大匙。

【作法】
❶ 猪蹄洗净，剁块，汆烫去血水。黄豆洗净、泡水约 1 小时。金针菜泡水备用。
❷ 锅内加适量水，放进全部材料，炖煮至肉烂、黄豆酥软加 (A) 料调味即可。

【Ingredients】
① 1 pig's foot ② 200g. soybean; 50g. dried day lily

【Seasoning】
(A) proper salt; 2 tbsp. wine

【Methods】
❶ Rinse and cut pig's foot into small pieces, then blanch. Rinse soybean and soak for 1 hour. Soak dry day lily.
❷ Put proper water, all the ingredients in a pot to stew until pig's foot and soybean are soft. Add seasoning (A) in.

【功效】
养血、通乳，可促进乳汁。

【Efficiency】
Make blood and help breast development.

淮杞羊肉汤
Stew Mutton with Yam and Wolfberry

【材料】
①带皮羊肉 500 克。
②山药 25 克、枸杞 10 克、桂圆肉 40 克、红枣 10 粒。
③老姜 1 块。

【调味料】
(A) 料：米酒 ½ 杯、盐适量。

【作法】
❶ 羊肉洗净、切块，余烫去血水。老姜切片。
❷ 炖锅内加水，放进羊肉，药材及姜片、米酒，煮开后，改小火熬煮至肉烂，加盐调味即可。

【Ingredients】
①500g. mutton ②25g. Chinese yam; 10g. fruit of Chinese wolfberry; 40g. dried longan; 10 red dates ③1 ginger.

【Seasoning】
(A) ½ cup of rice wine; proper salt

【Methods】
❶Rinse and cut mutton into small pieces. Blanch mutton in boiling water. Slice old ginger.
❷Stew mutton, herbage, sliced ginger, rice wine with some water. After boiling, turn to low heat to continue stewing until mutton is soft and done. Add salt in.

【功效】
健脾益气，温补肾阳，可治阳痿、早泄、腰膝酸软。
【Efficiency】
Good for spleen and kidney. Cure impotence and backache.

炒什锦

【材料】
素肉片··150 克
平菇··50 克
胡萝卜··½ 根
竹笋··½ 支
青花椰菜··½ 个
姜··2 片

【调味料】
高汤 ½ 杯、素蚝油 1 大匙、糖、酱油、香油各 1 小匙、盐少许、淀粉少许。

【作法】
❶ 青花椰菜洗净剥小朵，加 1 小匙盐，少许油入滚水中余烫。
❷ 平菇亦余烫备用。
❸ 起油锅，爆香姜末，接着放入香菇、肉片、笋片、胡萝卜片加少许高汤和调味料拌炒至入味，加入青花椰菜后勾薄芡，起锅前淋上香油即可。

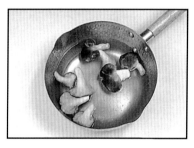

Fry Vegetables

【Ingredients】
150g. vegetarian meat slices, 50g. mini mushrooms,½ carrot, ½ bamboo shoot,½ green cauliflower, 2 pieces of ginger.

【Seasoning】
½ cup of broth, 1 tbsp. of vegetarian oyster sauce, 1 tbsp. of sugar and soy sauce, sesame oil, a dash of salt, cornstarch.

【Methods】
❶clean the green cauliflower and cut by pieces, add 1 tbsp. of salt, oil in boiling water and blanch.
❷Blanch the mini mushrooms.
❸Heat oil, sante chopped ginger, add black mushrooms, vegetarian meat slices, bamboo shoots slices, carrot slices, broth and spicies to fry, add green cauliflower and thicken, spread white sesame oil before turn off.

金银花丝瓜汤
Loofah Soup with Honeysuckle

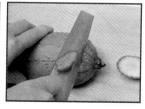

【材料】
① 丝瓜 1 条。
② 金银花 5 克、白果 50 克。
③ 嫩姜 1 块。
④ 蚬肉 100 克。

【调味料】
(A) 盐适量。

【作法】
❶ 丝瓜去皮，洗净，切片。金银花快速冲洗，沥干。白果泡软备用。嫩姜切片。蚬肉洗净、沥干。
❷ 锅内加水，先放入金银花、姜片、大火煮开后，改小火煮约 30 分钟后，放入丝瓜、白果与蚬肉，再煮约 25 分钟后，加(A) 料调味即可。

【Ingredients】
① 1 loofah ② 5g. honeysuckle; 50g. ginkgo seed. (Bai Guo) ③ 1 baby ginger. ④ 100g. shelled bivalves.

【Seasoning】
(A) proper salt

【Methods】
❶ Pare loofah, rinse and slice. Rinse honeysuckle and drain. Soak Bai Guo. Slice ginger. Rinse bivalves and drain.
❷ Cook honeysuckle and ginger with water. After boiling, turn to low heat to cook for 30 mins. then add loofah, Bai Guo and bivalves in and continue cooking for 25 mins, Add seasoning (A) in.

【功效】
清凉解毒、健胃、利尿、养颜美容。

【Efficiency】
Neutralize poison. Be diuretic. Good for stomach and skin.

冬瓜薏仁炖排骨
Stew Spareribs with Winter Melon and Yi Ren

【材料】
① 排骨 600 克。
② 冬瓜 1 块 (约500克)、薏仁 150 克。
③ 嫩姜 1 块。

【调味料】
(A) 料：盐适量。

【作法】
❶ 排骨洗净，余烫去血水。冬瓜去皮，切块。薏仁洗净，泡软。嫩姜切片。
❷ 锅内加水，将材料（除冬瓜外）全部放入，大火煮开后，转小火煮约 30分钟，再将冬瓜放入，煮至冬瓜软透，加(A) 料调味即可。

【Ingredients】
① 600g. sparerib ② 1 white gourd (about. 500g.); 150g. coix seed (Yi Ren) ③ 1 baby ginger

【Seasoning】
(A) proper salt

【Methods】
❶ Rinse and blanch spareribs in boiling water. Pare and cut white gourd into pieces. Rinse Yi Ren and soak until soft. Slice ginger.
❷ Cook all the ingredients except white gourd; after boiling, turn to low heat to continue cooking for 30 mins. then put white gourd in to cook until it's soft. Add seasoning (A) in.

【功效】
醒脾开胃，益气止痛、祛燥热。

【Efficiency】
Good for spleen and stomach. Nourish vitality and relieve heat.

参须红枣炖海扇
Stew Scallops with Ginsengs and Red Dates

【材料】
①海扇 250 克。
②鸡腿 1 只。
③参须 10～20 条，枸杞 5 克、红枣 8 粒。
④老姜 1 块。

【调味料】
(A) 料：酒 2 大匙、盐适量。

【作法】
❶ 海扇外壳刷洗干净。鸡腿剁块，余烫备用。药材稍冲洗，红枣泡软。老姜切片。
❷ 炖锅内加水，放入药材、姜片、鸡腿，大火煮开后，改小火煮约 30 分钟，再放入海扇，续煮约 30 分钟，加(A)料调味即可。

【Ingredients】
①250g. scallop ②1 chicken's leg ③10～12 pcs. of ginseng; 5g. fruit of Chinese wolfberry; 8 red dates ④1 ginger

【Seasoning】
(A) 2 tbsp. wine; proper salt.

【Methods】
❶Rinse the shell of scallops. Cut chicken's leg into small pieces, and blanch in boiling water. Rinse herbage. Soak red dates until soft. Slice ginger.
❷Put water, herbage, sliced ginger, chicken's leg in pot to cook with high heat; after boiling, turn to low heat to cook for 30 mins. then put scallops in to keep cooking for 30 mins. Add seasoning (A) in.

【功效】
补血益气、养肝明目。
【Efficiency】
Nourish vitality. Good for liver and eyes.

糖醋排骨

【材料】

芋头……………………………………½ 个
油条……………………………………2 条
菠萝……………………………………1 片
青椒……………………………………¼ 个
红椒……………………………………¼ 个
面粉……………………………………1 杯

【调味料】

低钠盐 2 小匙、糖 1 大匙、醋 1 大匙、番茄酱 2 大匙、香油 1 小匙、淀粉 2 大匙。

【作法】

❶ 芋头去皮洗净切细条，油条切小段，菠萝片、青椒、红椒均切丁。

❷ 芋头先用油炸过后，每段油条塞入 1 条芋头。

❸ 面粉加水调成糊状，再将油条一一沾面糊入 5 分热的油锅慢慢炸酥，捞出沥油。

❹ 起油锅，倒入菠萝丁、青椒丁、红椒丁略炒后盛起，将 ❸ 加入盐、糖、醋、番茄酱、水半杯焖煮至入味后，加菠萝、青椒、红椒丁稍拌炒后以水淀粉勾芡，淋上香油即可。

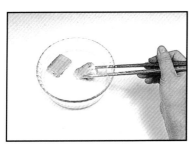

Sweet-Vinegar Rib

【Ingredients】

½ taro, 2 fried twisted dough sticks, 1 piece of pineapple, ¼ green bell pepper, ¼ red bell pepper, 1 cup of flour.

【Seasoning】

2 tbsp. of low sodium salt, 1 tbsp. of sugar, 1 tbsp. of vinegar, 2 tbsp. of ketchup, 1 tbsp. of white sesame oil, 2 tbsp. of cornstarch.

【Methods】

❶ Strip, clean and shred taro, cut the fried twisted dough stick by pieces, dice the pineapple, green bell pepper, red bell pepper.

❷ Fry the taro, then put the taro inside each of fried twisted dough stick.

❸ Stir flour with water into batter, coat the fried twisted dough stick by batter, and fry in the mid-heat oil, drain.

❹ Heat oil, fry the diced pineapple, green bell pepper, red bell papper, remove. Add salt, sugar, vinegar, ketchup, ½ cup of water in ❸ ingredients, stew until being well-done, and fry with pineapple, green and red bell pepper, thicken, spread white sesame oil.

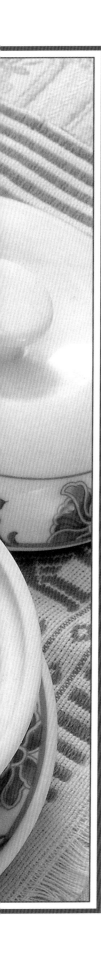

补脑汤
Stew Pig's Brain with Herbs

【材料】
① 猪脑 1 副。
② 山药 15 克、枸杞 5 克。

【调味料】
(A) 料：米酒 2 大匙、盐 1/2 茶匙。

【作法】
❶ 猪脑洗净，用牙签挑去外膜及血丝，汆烫去腥。山药、
枸杞泡水备用。

❷ 炖盅内加水、酒、猪脑及枸杞、山药等，放入电锅内，
锅内加水半杯，煮至开关跳起后，加盐调味即成。

【Ingredients】
① 1 pig's brain ② 15g. Chinese yam; 5g. fruit of Chinese
wolfberry.

【Seasoning】
(A) 2 tbsp. rice wine; ½ tbsp. salt

【Methods】
❶Rinse pig's brain, remove the membrane with a toothstick
and then blanch it in boiling water. Soak yam and fruit of
Chinese wolfberry.

❷Put water, wine, pig's brain, fruit of Chinese wolfberry,
yam in pot, and then put the pot in the electric cooker, pour
½ cup of water outside the pot. Add salt after the switch
turns off.

【功效】
补脑，安神宁心，增强抵抗力。

【Efficiency】
Good for brain. Calm down the mind. Increase immunity from disease.

四物鸡
Four Herbal Chicken

【材料】
① 乌骨鸡半只。
② 川芎15克、白芍20克、当归20克、熟地25克、枸杞15克。

【调味料】
(A) 料：米酒1杯。

【作法】
❶ 鸡去油脂，洗净，剁块，余烫去血水。药材快速冲洗沥干水分备用。
❷ 炖锅内加水、酒、鸡肉及药材，大火煮开后，改小火煮约1小时即可。

【Ingredients】
① ½ dark-skinned chicken ② 15g. rhizome of Chuanxiong; 20g. white paeonia (Bai Shao); 20g. angelica; 25g. root of Chinese foxglove (Shu Di Huang); 15g. fruit of Chinese wolfberry.

【Seasoning】
(A) 1 cup of rice wine.

【Methods】
❶ Clean and rinse chicken; and then cut into pieces and blanch in boiling water. Rinse herbage and drain.
❷ Put water, wine, chicken and herbage in pot to cook with high heat, after boiling, turn to low heat to cook for about 1 hour.

【功效】
补血益气，可促进血液循环，增强体力。

【Efficiency】
Nourish vitality. Improve blood circulation and increase energy.

党参红枣鸡
Stew Chicken with Dang Shen and Red Dates

【材料】
① 鸡1只。
② 党参50克、红枣150克。

【作法】
❶ 鸡去油脂，洗净，剁块，余烫去血水。红枣泡软。
❷ 炖锅内加水煮开，放入全部材料，小火炖约1小时即可。

【Ingredients】
① 1 free range chicken ② 50g. codonopsis pilosula (Dang Shen); 150g. red dates.

【Methods】
❶ Clean and rinse chicken; then cut into pieces and blanch in boiling water. Soak red dates.
❷ Put all the ingredients in boiling water to stew with low heat for 1 hour.

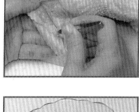

【功效】
补血益气，可治贫血、乏力、体虚。

【Efficiency】
Nourish vitality. Make blood. Cure anaemia, weak body.

苋菜豆腐羹

【材料】
苋菜250克、豆腐1块、鲜香菇5朵、荸荠6个、胡萝卜1块。

【调味料】
(A) 料：低钠盐2小匙、糖1小匙、素高汤5杯。
(B) 料：香油少许、胡椒粉少许、淀粉2大匙。

【作法】
❶ 苋菜洗净切碎，豆腐切细丁，鲜香菇去蒂切末。荸荠拍碎切末。
❷ 胡萝卜煮软，切细丁。
❸ 将素高汤注入锅中，加入豆腐、香菇、荸荠、胡萝卜，调味后煮约1分钟。
❹ 起锅前，放入苋菜勾芡，淋上香油、胡椒粉即可。

Amaranth Dou-Fu Soup

【Ingredients】
250g. amaranth, 1 cube of Dou-Fu, 5 black mushrooms, 6 water chestnuts, 1 cube of carrot.

【Seasoning】
(A) 2 tbsp. of low sodium salt, 1 tbsp. of sugar, 5 cups of vegetarian broth.
(B) white sesame oil, pepper, 2 tbsp. of cornstarch.

【Methods】
❶ Chean and chop the amaranth, cube the Dou-Fu, Cut the stems of black mushrooms off and chop. Chop the water chestnuts.
❷ Cook the carrot to be soft and dice.
❸ Add vegetarian broth in the pan, and add Dou-Fu, black mushrooms, water chestnuts, carrot, stew for 1 minute with spicies.
❹ Put the amaranth and thicken, spread white sesame oil, pepper before turn off.

酸辣汤

【材料】
豆腐1块、素火腿1块、香菇3朵、木耳2朵、竹笋½支、胡萝卜1小块、香菜、榨菜丝各少许。

【调味料】
低钠盐2小匙、糖1小匙、酱油1大匙、乌醋2小匙、胡椒少许、淀粉1大匙、香油1小匙。

【作法】
❶ 豆腐、素火腿切长条，香菇去蒂切丝，木耳、竹笋、胡萝卜均切丝。
❷ 起油锅，先爆香香菇，再将 ❷ 的材料全部入锅拌炒，然后注入适量的清水煮沸。加盐、糖、酱油、醋煮开，勾芡。
❸ 起锅前，淋香油，撒胡椒、香菜即可。

Spicy-Sour Soup

【Ingredients】
1 cube of Dou-Fu, 1 cube of vegetarian ham, 3 black mushrooms, 2 edible fungus, ½ bamboo shoot. 1 cube of carrot, parsley, salted mustard green.

【Seasoning】
2 tbsp. of low sodium salt, 1 tbsp. of sugar, 1 tbsp. of soy sauce, 2 tbsp. of black vinegar, pepper, 1 tbsp. of cornstarch, 1 tbsp. of white sesame oil.

【Methods】
❶ Cut the Dou-Fu and vegetarian ham into strings, cut the stem of balck mushroom and shred, shred edible fungus bamboo shoot, carrot.
❷ Heat oil, sante black mushroom, fry ❷ ingredients, and

add proper water until boiling, add salt, sugar, soy sauce, vinegar, and thicken.
❸ Spread white sesame oil, pepper, parsley before turn off.

章鱼炖猪蹄
Stew Pig's Hocks with Octopus

【材料】
①猪蹄4只。
②章鱼1条、姜1块、葱1根。

【调味料】
(A) 料：米酒2大匙、盐适量。

【作法】
❶ 猪蹄洗净，汆烫去血水。章鱼剥去外皮、洗净、切块。姜切片、葱切大段。
❷ 锅内加8杯水，放入全部材料及(A)料，煮至猪蹄酥软即可。

【Ingredients】
① 4 pig's hocks ② 1 octopus; 1 ginger; 1 scallion.

【Seasoning】
(A) 2 tbsp. rice wine; proper salt.

【Methods】
❶Rinse and blanch pig's hocks. Remove the membrane of octopus, rinse and cut into small pieces. Slice ginger. Cut scallion into sections.
❷Put 8 cups of water, all the ingredients and seasoning (A) in pot to stew until pig's hocks become soft.

【功效】
养血通乳。

【Efficiency】
Make blood and help breast development.

清炖羊肉
Stew Mutton

【材料】
①羊肉 500 克。
②萝卜 1 根、老姜 1 块、青蒜 1 根。
③红枣 8 粒、八角 1 粒。

【调味料】
(A) 料：米酒 1 杯、盐适量。

【作法】
❶ 羊肉洗净、切块，汆烫去腥。萝卜去皮、切块。老姜切片。青蒜切斜片。红枣泡软备用。
❷ 锅内加水、酒、药材及羊肉，大火煮开后，改小火煮约 1 小时后，再将萝卜加入，煮至肉烂，加盐及青蒜即可。

【Ingredients】
①500g. mutton ②1 radish; 1 ginger; 1 leek ③8 red dates; 1 Japanese star anise

【Seasoning】
(A) 1 cup of rice wine; proper salt.

【Methods】
❶Rinse and cut mutton into pieces; blanch. Pare and cube radish. Slice old ginger. Slice leek into section. Soak red dates.
❷Stew mutton with water, wine, and herbage, after boiling, turn to low heat to cook for 1 hour, and then add radish until mutton is soft and done. Add salt and leek in.

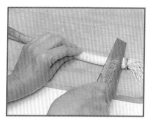

【功效】
益精补气、滋阴养血，可治腰膝酸软，手脚冰冷。

【Efficiency】
Nourish vitality. Make blood. Cure backache and cold limbs.

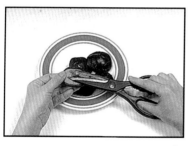

当归鸭

【材料】

素鸭……………………………………1 块
香菇……………………………………5 朵
当归……………………………………3 片
红枣…………………………………10 粒
枸杞………………………………1 大匙
白果…………………………………20 粒

【调味料】

(A) 料：酱油 1 大匙、香油少许。
(B) 料：低钠盐 2 小匙、米酒 4 大匙、素高汤 5 杯。

【作法】

❶ 素鸭以沸水煮约 3 分钟去油，红枣、枸杞洗净、白果浸水 1 小时，沥干备用，香菇泡软去蒂，以酱油、香油腌 10 分钟。

❷ 素鸭撕适口大小，连同所有材料放入炖盅内，加 (B) 料入锅，以大火蒸半小时即可。

Duck Seasoned with Angelica

【Ingredients】

1 vegetarian duck, 5 black mushrooms, 3 pieces of angelica, 10 red jujubes, 1 tbsp. of wolfberry, 20 ginkgo seed.

【Seasoning】

(A) 1 tbsp. of soy sauce, white sesame oil.
(B) 2 tbsp. of low sodium salt, 4 tbsp. of rice wine, 5 cups of vegetarian broth.

【Methods】

❶Cook the vegetarian duck in boiling water, keep the oil away, clean the red jujubes, wolfberry, soak the ginkgo seed in water for 1 hour, drain. Cut the stems of black mushrooms, keep them soft, pickle with soy sauce, white sesame oil for 10 minutes.

❷Tear the duck into proper size, put all ingredients in the stew pot, add (B) spicies, stew half an hour by high heat.

竹笋鲜菇汤

【材料】

竹笋⋯⋯⋯⋯⋯⋯⋯⋯⋯⋯⋯⋯⋯⋯⋯⋯⋯⋯75 克
香菇⋯⋯⋯⋯⋯⋯⋯⋯⋯⋯⋯⋯⋯⋯⋯⋯⋯⋯⋯8 朵
姜⋯⋯⋯⋯⋯⋯⋯⋯⋯⋯⋯⋯⋯⋯⋯⋯⋯⋯⋯1 小块
萝卜⋯⋯⋯⋯⋯⋯⋯⋯⋯⋯⋯⋯⋯⋯⋯⋯⋯⋯⋯1 根
芹菜⋯⋯⋯⋯⋯⋯⋯⋯⋯⋯⋯⋯⋯⋯⋯⋯⋯⋯⋯1 根

【调味料】

(A) 料：低钠盐 2 小匙、糖 1 小匙。
(B) 料：香油少许。

【作法】

❶ 香菇泡软去蒂，竹笋泡软切段，萝卜去皮切丝，芹菜切末。

❷ 爆香姜末、香菇、萝卜，再加竹笋、适量水及(A)料煮开，改小火煮约 15 分钟。

❸ 熄火前撒上芹菜末、香油即可。

Black Mushroom Soup with Bamboo Shoots

【Ingredients】

75g. bamboo shoots, 8 black mushroom, 1 cube of ginger, 1 radish, 1 celery.

【Seasoning】

(A) 2 tbsp. of low sodium salt, 1 tbsp. of sugar.
(B) white sesame oil.

【Methods】

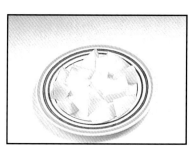

❶Cut the stems of black mushrooms and keep soft, soak and cut the bamboo shoots by pieces, strip and shred the radish, chop the celery.

❷Sante chopped ginger, black mushrooms, radish, add bamboo shoot, water and (A) spicies, stew by low heat for 15 minutes.

❸Spread chopped celery and white sesame oil before turn off.

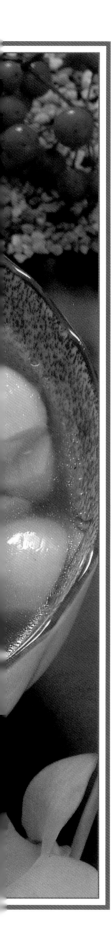

大蒜田鸡
Garlic Frogs

【材料】
① 田鸡 3 只。
② 大蒜 200 克、姜 1 块。
③ 枸杞 5 克。
【调味料】
(A) 料：米酒 2 大匙、盐适量。
【作法】
❶ 田鸡去皮、洗净、剁块、汆烫去血水。大蒜稍拍碎，姜切片。枸杞用开水冲一下。
❷ 锅内放水，放入全部材料煮开，改小火煮约 20 分钟，加(A) 料调味即可。

【Ingredients】
① 3 frog ② 200g. garlic; 1 ginger ③ 5g. fruit of Chinese wolfberry.
【Seasoning】
(A) 2 tbsp. rice wine; proper salt.
【Methods】
❶ Peel frogs, rinse and cut into pieces; blanch in boiling walter. Chop garlic; slice ginger. Wash fruit of Chinese wolfberry.
❷ Put water, all ingredients in pot to cook, after boiling, turn to low heat to cook for 20 mins. Add seasoning (A) in.

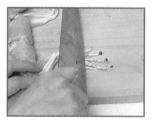

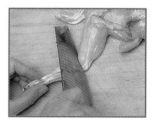

【功效】
清热解毒，利尿消肿、助消化。
【Efficiency】
Relieve heat; neutralize poison; reduce a swelling and help digestion.

发菜三丝汤
Sea Moss Soup

【材料】
① 发菜 25 克。
② 金针菇 200 克、熟笋 1 支、香菇 4 朵、香菜 1 棵、葱 1 根。
③ 高汤 8 杯。

【调味料】
(A) 盐 1/3 茶匙、糖 3/4 茶匙、陈醋、胡椒粉、香油各少许。
(B) 料：淀粉、水各少许。

【作法】
❶ 发菜洗净，泡水备用。金针菇去蒂，洗净。熟笋切丝。香菇泡软，洗净去蒂切丝。香菜切末，葱切段。
❷ 锅内放少许油，将葱段爆香后，加入高汤，烧开，将全部材料放入（除香菜外），煮约 10 分钟后，加 (A) 料调味后再加 (B) 料勾芡，起锅前加上香菜即可。

【Ingredients】
① 25g. sea moss ② 200g. dried day lily; 1 cooked bamboo shoot; 4 mushroom; 1 coriander; 1 scallion ③ 8 cups of broth.

【Seasoning】
(A) $1/3$ tbsp. salt; $3/4$ tbsp. sugar; a dash of black vinegar, pepper powder and sesame oil.
(B) a dash of cornstarch and water.

【Methods】
❶ Rinse and soak sea moss. Remove the stems of dried day lily and rinse. Shred bamboo shoot. Soak mushrooms, rinse and remove the stems. Mince coriander and cut scallion into sections.
❷ Fry scallion with a dash of oil until fragrant, and then add broth in to cook; put all the ingredients except coriander in while the broth is boiling, continue cooking for 10 mins. Add seasoning (A) and thicken with seasoning (B). Sprinkle coriander.

【功效】
补气、养血、养阴。

【Efficiency】
Nourish vitality. Make blood.

南杏排骨汤
Sparerib Soup with Nan Xing

【材料】
① 排骨 500 克。
② 南杏 150 克、水芹菜 100 克。

【调味料】
(A) 料：盐、香油各适量。

【作法】
❶ 排骨洗净、余烫去血水。水芹菜摘拣嫩叶，洗净备用。
❷ 锅内加水，放入排骨、南杏、大火煮开后，改小火煮至肉烂，再加入水芹菜、Ⓐ料调味即可。

【Ingredients】
① 500g. spareribs ② 150g. Nan Xing; 100g. water cress

【Seasoning】
(A) proper salt and sesame oil

【Methods】
❶ Rinse and blanch spareribs in boiling water. Remove the leaves of water cress and rinse.
❷ Cook spareribs, Nan Xing with water; after boiling, turn to low heat to continue cooking until spareribs are soft and done. Add water cress and seasoning (A) in.

【功效】
止咳、化痰、清肺、解热。

【Efficiency】
Stop coughing. Prevent phlegm from forming. Relieve heat.

三丝汤

【材料】

素丸子⋯⋯⋯⋯⋯⋯6 个
木耳⋯⋯⋯⋯⋯⋯⋯2 片
榨菜⋯⋯⋯⋯⋯⋯1 小块
胡萝卜⋯⋯⋯⋯⋯1 小块
素高汤⋯⋯⋯⋯⋯⋯1 罐

【调味料】

低钠盐2小匙、糖1小匙、胡椒粉少许。

【作法】

❶ 木耳、榨菜、胡萝卜均切丝。

❷ 适量高汤注入锅中煮开，加入素丸子、❶的材料及盐、糖煮熟。

❸ 起锅前撒些胡椒粉即可。

Three Ingredient Soup

【Ingredients】

6 vegetarian Meat ball, 2 pieces of edible fungus, 1 cube of pickled mustard tuber, 1 carrot, 1 jar of vegetarian broth.

【Seasoning】

2 tbsp. of low sodium salt, 1 tbsp. of sugar, pepper.

【Methods】

❶ Shred the edible fungus, Pickled mustard tuber, carrot.

❷ Cook the vegetarian broth, and the vegetarian meat ball, the ❶ingredients, salt, sugar.

❸ Spread pepper before turn off.

火腿玉米浓汤

【材料】

素火腿⋯⋯⋯⋯⋯⋯1 块
玉米酱⋯⋯⋯⋯⋯⋯1 罐
鲜香菇⋯⋯⋯⋯⋯⋯2 朵
牛奶⋯⋯⋯⋯⋯⋯⋯适量

【调味料】

低钠盐2小匙、糖1小匙、水适量、淀粉2大匙、胡椒粉少许。

【作法】

❶ 鲜香菇去蒂、素火腿切丁备用。

❷ 起油锅，爆香❶后，加入玉米酱拌匀。

❸ 适量水入❷的锅中煮开后加上盐及糖调味，勾芡。加入少许牛奶，起锅前撒些胡椒粉即可。

Ham Corn Soup

【Ingredients】

1 cube of vegetarian ham, 1 jar of corn jam, 2 black mushrooms, proper milk.

【Seasoning】

2 tbsp. of low sodium salt, 1 tbsp. of sugar, water, 2 tbsp. of cornstarch, pepper.

【Methods】

❶Cut the stem of black mushroom off, dice the vegetarian ham.

❷heat oil, sante the ❶ingredients, stir with corn jam.

❸Add water in ❷and put salt, sugar, thicken, then add milk, spread pepper before turn off.

当归鲶鱼
Stew Bullhead with Angelica

【材料】
①鲶鱼 1 条。
②当归 3 片、黄芪 10 克、枸杞 7.5 克。
③老姜 1 块、紫苏少许。

【调味料】
(A) 料：米酒半杯、盐适量。

【作法】
❶ 鲶鱼去内脏、洗净。药材快速冲洗干净，沥干，备用。
老姜切片，紫苏洗净。
❷ 炖锅内加适量水，将鲶鱼、药材、姜片、米酒加入，煮
开后改小火炖煮约 1 小时，加盐调味，食用时加上紫苏
则更加美味。

【Ingredients】
① 1 catfish ② 3 slices of angelica root; 10g. astragalus
membranaceus (Huang Qi); 7.5g. fruit of Chinese wolfberry
③ 1 ginger; a dash of basil

【Seasoning】
(A) ½ cup of rice wine; proper salt.

【Methods】
❶Remove the viscera of catfish; rinse. Rinse herbage; drain.
Slice ginger; rinse basil.
❷Put proper water, catfish, herbage, sliced ginger and rice
wine in pot to stew. after boiling, turn to low heat to cook
for 1 hour; add salt. Add basil before eating, the taste will
be better.

【功效】
利水消肿，清热解毒，滋阴补虚。
【Efficiency】
Reduce a swelling; relieve heat; neutralize poison; nourish vitality.

猪肚炖莲子
Stew Pig's Tripe with Lotus Seeds

【材料】
① 猪肚 1 个。肉片 100 克。
② 莲子 200 克。
③ 萝卜 1 根、嫩姜 1 块。

【调味料】
(A) 料：酱油 1 大匙、淀粉、水各少许。
(B) 料：米酒 2 大匙、盐、香油适量。

【作法】
❶ 猪肚洗净，氽烫后切片。肉片加(A) 料腌 10 分钟。莲子洗净，泡水。萝卜去皮切块。嫩姜切丝。
❷ 锅内加水，放入莲子、猪肚煮约 30 分钟后，再将萝卜、姜丝放入，煮至莲子、猪肚、萝卜熟烂，再投入肉片、(B) 料，稍煮一下即可。

【Ingredients】
① 1 pig's tripe; 100g. sliced meat ②200g. lotus seeds ③1 radish; 1 baby ginger.

【Seasoning】
(A) 1 tbsp. soy sauce; a dash of cornstarch and water.
(B) 2 tbsp. rice wine; proper salt and sesame oil.

【Methods】
❶Rinse pig's tripe, blanch and then cut into pieces. Marinate sliced meat in seasoning (A) for 10 mins. Rinse lotus seeds and soak. Pare and cube radish. Shred ginger.
❷Stew lotus seeds, pig's tripe with water for 30 mins. and then add radish, ginger to continue cooking until lotus seeds, pig's tripe and radish are soft; add sliced meat, seasoning (B) to cook for a while.

【功效】
健脾益胃，可治体虚、乏力。
【Efficiency】
Good for spleen and stomach. Strengthen the body.

熏鹅

【材料】

豆腐皮·······························6 张
香菇·······························4 朵
金针菇·······························100 克
胡萝卜·······························1 根
姜·······························1 块
香菜·······························1 根

【调味料】

(A) 料：酱油 1 大匙、胡椒粉、糖、香油各少许。

(B) 料：低钠盐 1 小匙、酱油 1 小匙、糖、香油、姜末各少许。

【作法】

❶ 香菇泡软切丝，金针菇余烫、胡萝卜切丝、香菜切长段。

❷ 起油锅，先爆香香菇再放金针菇、胡萝卜丝、香菜段、(B) 料炒匀。

❸ 备一长盘，中间、两旁各置放 2 张豆皮，淋入(A) 料后平铺炒好的馅料，并卷成长形，放入蒸锅蒸 3 分钟后，即可取出待凉。

* 熏鹅作法：

炒菜锅内先放 1 张锡箔纸、150 克红砂糖、再放蒸架（不放水）中火熏 3 分钟即可。

Smoked Goose

【Ingredients】

6 pieces of dry bean curd, 4 black mushrooms, 100g. golden mushrooms, 1 carrot, 1 cube of ginger, 2 parsley.

【Seasoning】

(A) 1 tbsp. of soy sauce, pepper, sugar, white sesame oil.

(B) 1 tbsp. of low sodium salt, 1 tbsp. of soy sauce, sugar, white sesame oil, chopped ginger.

【Methods】

❶Soak the black mushrooms and shred, blanch the golden mushrooms. Shred carrot, cut parsley into sections.

❷Heat oil, sante black mushrooms, add golden mushrooms, carrot, parsley and (B) spicies.

❸Put 4 pieces of dry bean curd in the middle and two sides of plate, add (A) spicies, put the fried ingredients, wrap into long shape, steam for 3 minutes, cool it down.

*Smoked Goose:

Put one piece of tinfoil paper on the pan, 150g. red granulated sugar, put the steam pan on (no-water) stove, smoke for 3 minutes by mid-heat.

锁阳山药炖鸡汤
Stew Rooster with Suo Yang and Yam

【材料】
① 公鸡半只。
② 党参、山药各 15 克、锁阳、金樱子各 10 克、北五味子 7.5 克。

【作法】
❶ 公鸡去油脂，洗净，剁块，氽烫去血水。药材快速冲洗后沥干。
❷ 炖锅内加水煮开，放进鸡肉、药材、小火炖约 2 小时即可。

【Ingredients】
① ½ rooster ② 15g. each of codonopsis pilosula (Dang Shen) and Chinese yam; 10g. each of Cynomorium songaricum Rupr. (Suo Yang) and Rosa laevigata Mickx. (Jin Ying Zi); 7.5g. Schisandra fruit (Bei Wu Wei Zi).

【Methods】
❶ Clean and rinse rooster, cut into pieces and then blanch in boiling water. Rinse all herbage, drain.
❷ Put rooster, herbage in boiling water to stew with low heat for about. 2 hours.

【功效】
补肾壮阳，可治阳痿、早泄。
【Efficiency】
Good for kidney. Cure impotence.

四神汤
Four Herbal Soup

【材料】
① 猪肠 500 克。
② 莲子 150 克、山药、茯苓、芡实各 25 克、薏仁 150 克。

【调味料】
(A) 料：米酒 2 大匙、盐适量。

【作法】
❶ 猪肠剪去油脂，用面粉搓洗干净，翻面，再用醋洗净粘液后氽烫备用。莲子洗净，泡水。其他药材快速冲洗后沥干水份。
❷ 锅内加水煮开，放入猪肠、酒及全部药材，煮至猪肠熟烂，加盐调味即可。

【Ingredients】
① 500g. pig's intestine ② 150g. lotus seeds; 25g. each of Chinese yam, tuckahoe, gorgon fruit; 150g. coix seed (Yi Ren).

【Seasoning】
(A) 2 tbsp. rice wine; proper salt.

【Methods】
❶ Clean pig's intestine and rinse with flour; reverse, and rinse to remove mucus with vinegar; blanch. Rinse and soak lotus seeds. Rinse all herbage; drain.
❷ Put pig's intestine, wine and all herbage in boiling water to cook until pig's intestine is soft and done. Add salt in.

【功效】
补脾益气、健胃。可治食欲不振，消化不良。
【Efficiency】
Good for spleen and stomach. Nourish vitality. Cure bad appetite and help digestion.

当归鸭
Stew Duck with Angelica

【材料】
①鸭 1 只。
②川芎 10 克、黄芪 20 克、枸杞 10 克、桂枝 15 克、当归 20 克。

【调味料】
(A) 料：米酒半杯、盐适量。

【作法】
❶ 鸭去杂质、洗净、剁块、汆烫去血水。药材快速冲洗备用。
❷ 将鸭肉、药材和酒全放进炖锅内，加水煮开后，改小火炖煮至肉烂，加盐调味即可。

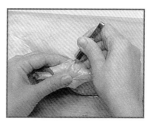

【Ingredients】
① 1 duck ② 10g. rhizome of Chuanxiong; 20g. astragalus membranaceus (Huang Qi); 10g. fruit of Chinese wolfberry; 15g. ramulus Cinnamomi (Gui Zhi); 20g. angelica root.

【Seasoning】
(A) ½ cup of rice wine; Proper salt.

【Methods】
❶ Clean and rinse duck, cut it into small pieces and blanch in boiling water. Rinse herbage.
❷ Put duck, herbage, wine and water in pot to cook until boiling, and then turn to low heat to stew. Add salt in when duck is soft and done.

【功效】
补气血，去水肿、润燥利肠，美容养颜。
【Efficiency】
Nourish vitality; remove edema; moisten intestines.

茄汁豆泡

【材料】
豆腐泡·····················6个
鲜香菇·····················4朵
胡萝卜·····················½根
青椒······················1个
香菜······················1根
姜·······················1小块

【调味料】
低纳盐1小匙、番茄酱1大匙、糖1小匙、香油1大匙、素高汤2碗。

【作法】
❶ 胡萝卜去皮切丝，青椒去籽切丝，鲜香菇去蒂切丝。
❷ 起油锅，先爆香香菇、姜末，再放入胡萝卜、青椒同炒，接着注入2碗素高汤、豆腐泡、盐、番茄酱、糖焖煮5分钟，待入味后勾芡，起锅前淋上香油、香菜即可食用。

Dry Bean Stuffed Bun with Eggplant Sauce

【Ingredients】
6 dry bean stuffed bun, 4 fresh black mushrooms, ½ carrot, 1 green bell pepper, 1 parsley, 1 cube of ginger.

【Seasoning】
1 tbsp. of low sodium salt, 2 tbsp. of ketchup, 1 tbsp. of sugar, 1 tbsp. of white sesame oil, 2 bowls of vegetarian broth.

【Methods】
❶ Strip and shred carrot, keep the seeds away and shred green bell pepper, cut the stems and shred black mushrooms.
❷ Heat oil, sante black mushrooms, chopped ginger, add carrot, green bell pepper to fry, pour 2 bowls of broth, dry bean stuffed bun, salt, ketchup, sugar to stew for 5 minutes, thicken, spread white sesame oil, parsley before turn off.

胡萝卜猪尾汤
Pig's Tail Soup with Carrot

【材料】
① 猪尾 1 条。
② 胡萝卜 1 根、马铃薯 2 个、香菜 2 棵。

【调味料】
(A) 料：盐适量。

【作法】
❶ 猪尾洗净，切段，余烫去血水。胡萝卜、马铃薯去皮，切滚刀块。香菜切段。
❷ 锅内加水，放入猪尾，先煮约 40 分钟后，再放入胡萝卜及马铃薯，再煮至猪尾熟烂，加 (A) 料调味后再撒入香菜即可。

【Ingredients】
① 1 pig's tail ② 1 carrot; 2 potato; 2 coriander.

【Seasoning】
(A) proper salt

【Methods】
❶ Rinse pig's tail and cut into small sections; blanch in boiling water. Pare carrot and potatoes; cube. Cut coriander into small sections.
❷ Put water and pig's tail in pot to cook for 40 mins. then add carrot and potatoes to continue cooking until pig's tail is soft and done. Add seasoning (A) and sprinkle coriander.

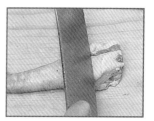

【功效】
养肝明目，健胃消食。
【Efficiency】
Good for liver, eyes and stomach.

粉光参炖猪心
Stew Pig's Heart with Fen Guang Shen

【材料】

①猪心 1 个。

②粉光参 15 克，当归、枸杞、杜仲各 10 克。黄芪 20 克。红枣 8 粒。

【调味料】

(A) 料：米酒 1 瓶、盐适量。

【作法】

❶ 猪心挤去血水，洗净，氽烫备用。药材快速冲洗沥干备用。

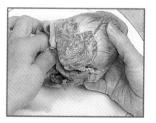

❷ 炖锅内加水及酒，将全部药材、猪心放入，煮开后改小火煮约 1 小时即可。(可视个人需要加盐调味)

【Ingredients】

①1 pig's heart ②15g. panar quinquefolium L. (Fen Guang Shen); 10g. each of angelica root, fruit of Chinese wolfberry and eucommia bark (Du Zhong); 20g. astragalus membranaceus (Huang Qi); 8 red dates.

【Seasoning】

(A) 1 bottle of rice wine; proper salt.

【Methods】

❶Clean, rinse and blanch pig's heart. Rinse herbage; drain.

❷Stew all the herbage, pig's heart, wine with water. After boiling, turn to low heat to cook for 1 hour. (Adding salt depends on one's favor.)

【功效】

补血、安神、增强体力。

【Efficiency】

Make blood. Calm down the minds. Increase energy.

莲子百合瘦肉汤
Lean Soup with Lotus Seeds and Lily Bulb

【材料】
① 小里脊 300 克。
② 莲子 200 克、百合 50 克。
③ 葱 1 根。
④ 高汤 8 杯。

【调味料】
(A) 料：盐 1/4 茶匙、香油少许、淀粉、水各适量。
(B) 料：盐、香油适量。

【作法】
❶ 小里肌洗净，切片，加(A)料腌 10 分钟。莲子、百合泡软。葱切段。
❷ 锅内加入高汤，先将莲子、百合煮软，再将肉片一一投入，加上葱段和(B)料即可。

【Ingredients】
① 300g. lean ② 200g. lotus seed; 50g. lily bulb ③ 1 scallion ④ 8 cups of broth.

【Seasoning】
(A) 1/4 tbsp. salt; a dash of sesame oil; proper cornstarch and water.
(B) proper salt and sesame oil.

【Methods】
❶ Rinse and slice lean; then marinate lean in seasoning (A) for 10 mins. Soak lotus seeds and lily bulb. Cut scallion into small sections.
❷ Cook lotus seeds and lily bulbs with broth. When lotus seeds and lily bulbs are soft and done, put sliced lean; add scallion and seasoning (B).

【功效】
健脾补肾、安神。可治失眠、头痛。

【Efficiency】
Good for spleen and kidney. Calm down the mind. Cure insomnia and headache.

- -

玉米须炖蚌肉
Stew Calms with Corn Silk

【材料】
① 玉米须 15 克。
② 兰花蚌 300 克。
③ 葱 1 根、嫩姜 1 块。

【调味料】
(A) 料：盐、香油适量。

【作法】
❶ 玉米须、蚌肉皆洗净备用。葱洗净切段，嫩姜切段。
❷ 锅内加水，将玉米须放入，大火煮开后，改小火煮约 30 分钟，再将姜丝、葱段、蚌肉放入，稍煮，加(A)料调味即可。

【Ingredients】
① 15g. cornsilk. (Yu Mi Xu) ② 300g. shelled clams ③ 1 scallion; 1 baby ginger.

【Seasoning】
(A) proper salt, sesame oil.

【Methods】
❶ Rinse corn silk and clams. Rinse and cut scallion into small sections. Shred baby ginger.
❷ Put some water, corn silk in pot to cook with high heat. after boiling, turn to low heat to cook for 30 mins. put ginger, scallion, clams in to continue cooking for a while. Add seasoning (A).

【功效】
平肝利胆，清热降血压。

【Efficiency】
Good for liver and gallbladder. Relieve heat and lower blood pressure.

凉拌西芹

【材料】
西洋芹……………………1 棵
红辣椒……………………1 根
【调味料】
低钠盐 2 小匙、香油 3 小匙。
【作法】
❶ 西洋芹汆烫后，撕掉外层粗丝，切小段。
❷ 红辣椒洗净切丝，与调味料一起加入西洋芹中拌匀，置于冰箱冰凉即可。

Cold Dressed Celery

【Ingredients】
1 banch of celery, 1 red chilli.
【Seasoning】
2 tbsp. of low sodium salt, 3 tbsp. of white sesame oil.
【Methods】
❶Blanch the celery, tear the skins, cut it by pieces.
❷ Clean and shred the red chilli, add in the celery with spicies, put them in the refrigerator.

凉拌干丝

【材料】
豆腐丝………………200 克
胡萝卜…………………¼ 根
芹菜……………………3 棵
【调味料】
低钠盐 2 小匙、香油 3 小匙、辣油适量。
【作法】
❶ 豆腐丝洗净，胡萝卜洗净去皮切丝，芹菜去叶洗净切段。
❷ 豆腐丝放入沸水煮 3 分钟后捞出，浸于冷开水中，沥去水分盛盘。
❸ 胡萝卜丝和芹菜段放入热水中汆烫，待凉后拌入豆腐丝中，加调味料拌匀即可。

Cold Dressed Dried Bean Curd Shredded

【Ingredients】
200g. Dried bean curd shredded, ¼ carrot, 3 celery.
【Seasoning】
2 tbsp. of low soduim salt, 3 tbsp. of white sesame oil, a dash of spicy oil.
【Methods】
❶Clean the dried bean curd shredded, strip and shred carrot, celery no leaves and cut into sections.
❷ Stew the dried bean curd shredded in boiling water for about 3 minutes, then cool by cold water, drain up and put on a plate.
❸Blanch the carrot and celery, cool them down, add the dried bean curd shredded and spicies, mix them well.

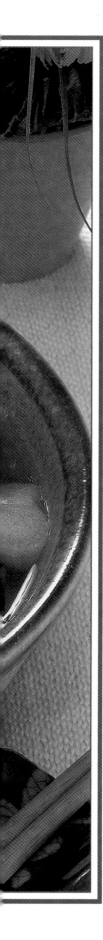

竹笋香菇鸡
Black Mushroom Chicken with Bamboo Shoots

【材料】
① 鸡半只。
② 竹笋 15 克、香菇 6 朵、姜 1 块、葱 1 根。

【调味料】
(A) 料：酒 2 大匙、盐适量。

【作法】
❶ 鸡去油脂，洗净，剁块，余烫去血水。竹笋泡水、去杂质。香菇泡软、切大片。姜切片。葱切两段。
❷ 炖锅内加水，将全部材料放进，煮开后，改小火炖煮至肉烂，加(A)料调味即可。

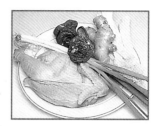

【Ingredients】
①½ chicken ②15g. bamboo shoot; 6 mushroom; 1 ginger; 1 scallion.

【Seasoning】
(A) 2 tbsp. wine; proper salt

【Methods】
❶Clean and rinse chicken, then cut into small pieces and blanch in boiling water. Soak bamboo shoot and remove impurity. Soak mushrooms and slice. Slice ginger. Cut scallion into two sections.
❷Put all the ingredients and water in pot to cook, after boiling turn to low heat to stew until chicken is soft and done. Add seasoning (A).

【功效】
增强体力，滋润气色，消除疲劳。
【Efficiency】
Nourish vitality; eliminate fatigue.

山药百合炖鳗鱼

Stew River Eel with Yam and Lily Bulb

【材料】
①鳗鱼1条。
②山药40克、百合25克、枸杞10克。

【调味料】
(A) 料：米酒半杯、盐适量。

【作法】
❶ 鳗鱼去内脏、洗净。枸杞快速冲洗，沥干备用，山药百合泡水。

❷ 炖锅内加水，将鳗鱼与药材、米酒一起放入，煮开后改小火炖约30分钟，加盐调味即可。

【Ingredients】
①1 river eel ②40g. Chinese yam; 25g. lily bulb; 10g. fruit of Chinese wolfberry.

【Seasoning】
(A) ½ cup of rice wine; proper salt.

【Methods】
❶Remove the viscera of eel and rinse. Rinse fruit of Chinese wolfberry and drain. Soak Yam and lily bulb.

❷Stew eel, herbage, rice wine with water, after boiling, turn to low heat to stew for 30 mins. Add salt.

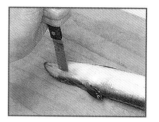

【功效】
健脾补气，清心宁神，增强体力。

【Efficiency】
Good for spleen. Nourish vitality and increase vigor.

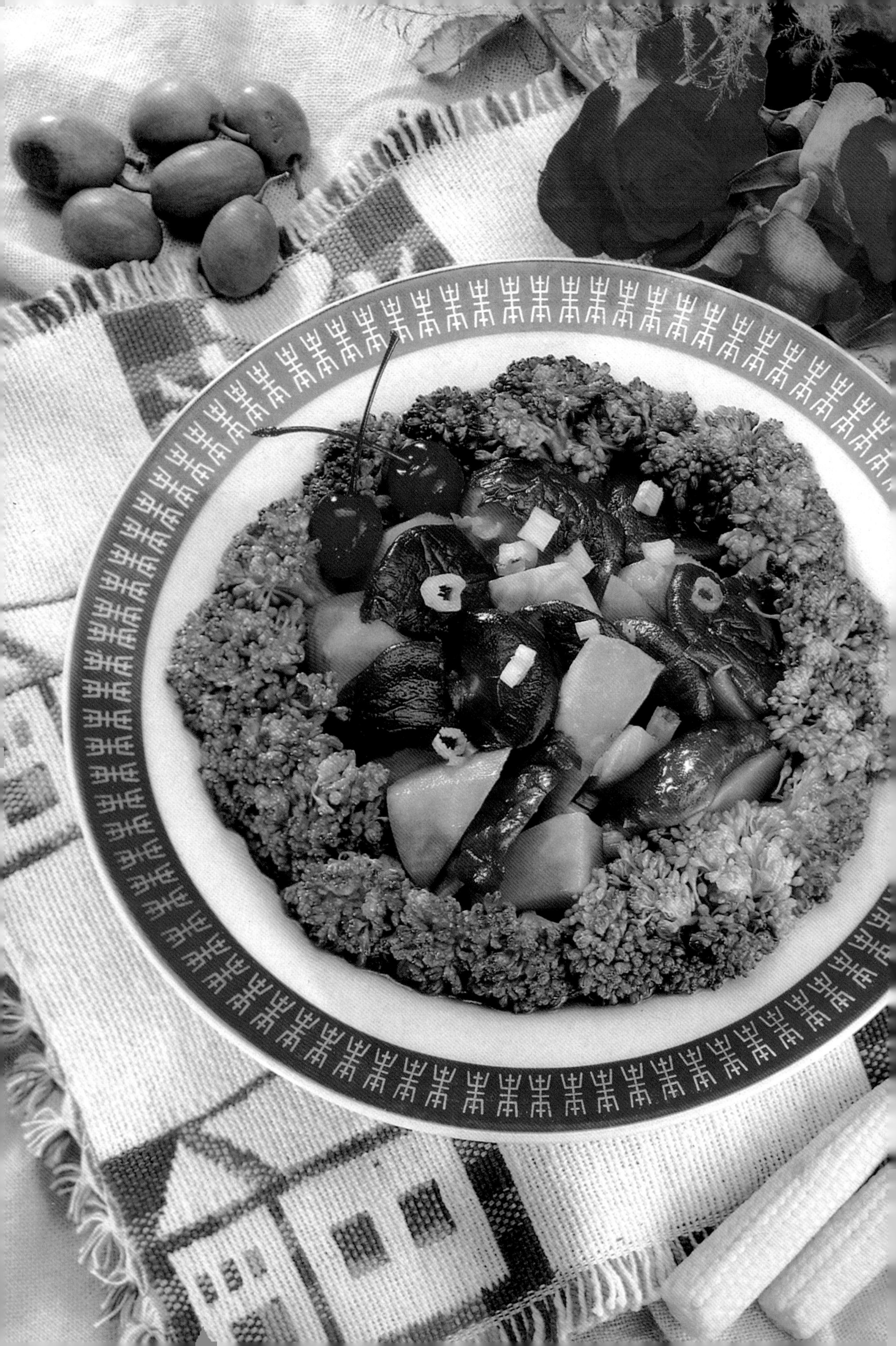

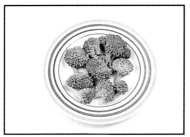

烩双冬

【材料】
冬菇·····························8 朵
冬笋·····························1 根
芹菜·····························2 根
青花椰菜·····························1 棵

【调味料】
(A) 料：低钠盐、糖、香油各 1 小匙、蚝油 2 大匙。
(B) 料：淀粉 1 大匙。

【作法】
❶ 冬菇去蒂斜切成半，冬笋切块，芹菜去叶切末。
❷ 热油，将冬菇、冬笋入锅略炸，捞出沥油备用。
❸ 另起油锅，冬菇、冬笋与(A) 料入锅稍焖后勾薄芡，起锅前撒下芹菜末即可。

Fry Mushrooms with Bamboo Shoots

【Ingredients】
8 black mushrooms, 1 bamboo shoot, 2 celery, 1 green cauliflower.

【Seasoning】
(A) 1 tbsp. each of low sodium salt, sugar, white sesame oil, 2 tbsp. of vegetarian oyster sauce.
(B) 1 tbsp. of cornstarch.

【Methods】
❶Cut the stems of mushrooms off and cut into halves, cube the bamboo shoot, chop the no-leaves celery.
❷Heat oil, fry the black mushrooms, bamboo shoots, and drain up.
❸Heat another oil, stir black mushrooms, bamboo shoots with (A) spicies, stew for a few minutes, thicken, spread chopped celery before turn off.

川芎鱼头汤
Grass Carp Soup with Chuan Xiong

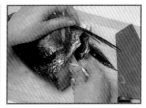

【材料】
① 草鱼头 1 个。
② 川芎 15 克、白芷 5 克、当归 2 片、红枣 10 粒、枸杞 10 克。
③ 青蒜 1 根。

【调味料】
(A)料：酒 1 大匙、盐、香油适量。

【作法】
❶ 鱼头去鳃、鳞、洗净。药材快速冲洗，沥干备用。青蒜洗净，切斜片。
❷ 锅内加水，将药材放入，煮开后，转小火煮约 20 分钟，再放入鱼头，煮约 40 分钟，加(A)料调味撒上青蒜即可。

【Ingredients】
① 1 head of grass carp ② 15g. rhizome of Chuan Xiong; 5g. dahuri an angelica root (Bai Zhi); 2 slices of angelica; 10 red dates; 10g. fruit of Chinese wolfberry ③ 1 leek.

【Seasoning】
(A) 1 tbsp. wine; proper salt and sesame oil.

【Methods】
❶ Remove the gill, scale of carp and then rinse. Rinse herbage; drain. Rinse and slice leek diagonally.
❷ Cook herbage with water, after boiling, turn to low heat to cook for 30 mins. and then put head of grass carp in to continue cooking for more 40 mins. Add seasoning (A) and sprinkle leek.

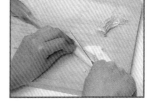

【功效】
补血利肠、养脑。
【Efficiency】
Make blood. Good for intestines and brain.

水芹菜鱼片汤
Sliced Grass Carp Soup with Water Cress

【材料】
① 草鱼 300 克。
② 水芹菜 150 克、嫩姜 1 块。
③ 高汤 7 杯。

【调味料】
(A)料：盐 ¼ 茶匙、酒 1 茶匙、水淀粉少许。
(B)料：酒 1 大匙、盐、香油、胡椒粉适量。

【作法】
❶ 草鱼切片，加(A)料腌 10 分钟。水芹菜摘拣嫩叶，洗净。嫩姜切丝。
❷ 锅内放高汤，煮开后将水芹菜、嫩姜与鱼片放入，再煮开，加(B)料调味即可。

【Ingredients】
① 300g. grass carp ② 150g. water cress; 1 baby ginger ③ 7 cups of broth.

【Seasoning】
(A) ¼ tbsp. salt; 1 tbsp. wine; a dash of cornstarch solution
(B) 1 tbsp. wine; proper salt, sesame oil and pepper powder

【Methods】
❶ Slice grass carp, and then marinate in seasoning (A) for 10 mins. Remove the leaves of water cress and rinse. Shred baby ginger.
❷ Cook broth and after boiling, put water cress, ginger and grass carp to continue cooking until boiling. Add seasoning (B).

【功效】
健胃、祛风、退火、解热。
【Efficiency】
Good for stomach. Relieve heat.

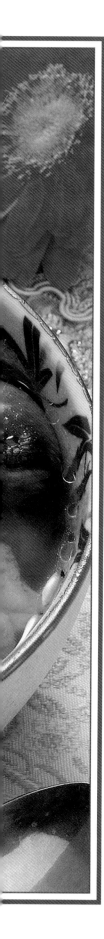

栗子鸡汤
Stew Chicken with Chestnut

【材料】
① 鸡半只。
② 栗子 250 克。
③ 大蒜 100 克。

【调味料】
(A) 盐适量。

【作法】
❶ 鸡去杂质，洗净，剁块，氽烫去血水。栗子洗净，用热水泡软后，剥去外壳、皮膜。大蒜去蒂，洗净。
❷ 锅内放水，烧开，先将栗子放进煮约40分钟，再将鸡肉放入，煮至栗子、鸡肉松软加盐调味即可。

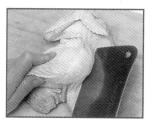

【Ingredients】
① ½ chicken ② 250g. chestnut ③ 100g. garlic

【Seasoning】
(A) proper salt

【Methods】
❶Clean, rinse and cut chicken into pieces, blanch in boiling water. Rinse chestnuts and soak them in hot water until becoming soft, pare. Remove the stems of garlic and then rinse.
❷Put chestnuts in boiling water to cook for about. 40 mins. then add chicken. Add salt when chestnuts and chicken are soft and done.

【功效】
补中益气，滋阴补肾，强筋骨，活血路。
【Efficiency】
Nourish vitality; strengthen the body; help blood circulation.

烩海参

【材料】

素海参·····································2 条
竹笋·····································2 根
胡萝卜································½ 根
红辣椒·····························1 根
香菇·····································4 朵

【调味料】

低钠盐2小匙、酱油2大匙、糖2小匙、水淀粉2大匙、香油1小匙。

【作法】

❶ 素海参以盐水氽烫后切段，竹笋去皮洗净切片，胡萝卜削皮洗净切片，红辣椒切丝，香菇泡水斜切成3片。

❷ 热3大匙油爆香辣椒丝及香菇，放入素海参略炒后加入竹笋片、胡萝卜片续炒。

❸ 将盐、酱油、糖、水调匀后，倒入❷锅中焖煮。待汤汁快干时，以水淀粉勾芡淋上香油即可。

Braise Trepang

【Ingredients】

2 trepang, 2 bamboo shoots, ½ carrot, 1 red chilli, 4 mushrooms.

【Seasoning】

2 tbsp. of low sodium salt, 2 tbsp. of soy sauce, 2 tbsp. of sugar, 2 tbsp. of cornstarch water, 1 tbsp. of white sesame oil.

【Methods】

❶ blanch and cut the trepang by pieces, clean,strip and slice the bamboo shoots, carrot. Shredded red chilli, soak the mushroom in water and trisect it.

❷ Heat oil, sante red chilli and mushroom, add trepang, bamboo shoots, carrot, continue to fry.

❸ Mix with salt, soy sauce, sugar, water, put them in ❷ and stew. Until the soup going to dry, thicken by cornstarch water, spread white sesame oil.

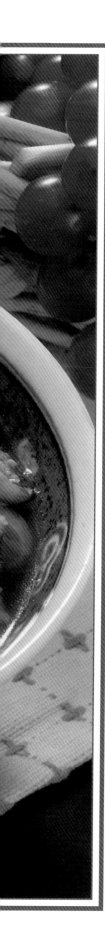

当归羊肉汤
Stew Mutton with Angelica

【材料】
① 带皮羊肉 500 克。
② 当归 40 克、黄芪 15 克、红枣 8 粒、桂圆肉 20 克、八角 1 粒。
③ 葱 1 根、老姜 1 块。

【调味料】
(A) 料：米酒 2 大匙、盐适量。

【作法】
❶ 羊肉洗净，切块，余烫去腥。葱切段、老姜切片。药材快速冲洗沥干备用。
❷ 锅内加水，将全部材料、酒放入，煮开后转小火煮至肉烂，加盐调味即可。

【Ingredients】
① 500g. mutton ② 40g. angelice, 15g. astragalus membranaceus (Huang Qi), 8 red dates; 20g. dry longan, 1 Japanese star anise ③ 1 scallion, 1 ginger.

【Seasoning】
(A) 2 tbsp. rice wine; proper salt.

【Methods】
❶Rinse mutton, cut into pieces and blanch. Cut scallion into small sections.slice ginger, Rinse herbage; drain.
❷Stew all the ingredients, wine with water. After boiling, turn to low heat until mutton is soft and done. Add salt.

【功效】
调经、补血、补气、可治贫血，头昏目眩。
【Efficiency】
Make blood, Cure anemia. Regulate menses.

肉苁蓉猪肝汤
Pig's Liver Soup with Rou Cong Rong

【材料】
①猪肝 300 克。
②肉苁蓉 20 克。

【调味料】
(A) 料：盐适量。

【作法】
❶ 猪肝洗净，切片。肉苁蓉洗净，切片。
❷ 锅内加水，放入肉苁蓉，先煮约 30 分种，再放入猪肝，煮熟，加(A) 料调味即可。

【Ingredients】
① 300g. pig's liver ② 20g. cistanche salsa (Rou Cong Rong)

【Seasoning】
(A) proper salt

【Methods】
❶ Rinse and slice pig's liver and rou cong rong
❷ Cook rou cong rong with water for about 30 mins. and then put pig's liver to cook until it is well done. Add seasoning (A).

【功效】
生精补血，益气补虚。

【Efficiency】
Nourish vitality. Make blood.

. . . .

首乌枸杞炖鸡汤
Stew Chicken with He Shou Wu

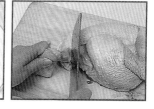

【材料】
①鸡半只。
②首乌 40 克、枸杞 15 克。

【调味料】
(A) 料：盐适量。

【作法】
❶ 鸡去油脂，洗净，剁块，余烫去血水。药材冲洗，沥干。
❷ 炖锅内加水，放入鸡肉与药材，大火煮开后，转小火炖至肉烂加(A) 料调味即可。

【Ingredients】
① ½ free range chicken ② 40g. polygonum multiflorum (He Shou Wu); 15g. fruit of Chinese wolfberry.

【Seasoning】
(A) proper salt

【Methods】
❶ Rinse and clean chicken, cut it into pieces and then blanch in boiling water. Rinse herbage and drain.
❷ Cook chicken and herbage with water, after boiling, turn to low heat to stew until chicken is soft. Add seasoning (A).

【功效】
补血益气。可治血虚、头晕。

【Efficiency】
Make blood. Nourish vitality. Cure headache.

117

凉拌小黄瓜

【材料】
小黄瓜·····················5 条
红辣椒·····················1 根
白芝麻·····················少许

【调味料】
低钠盐2小匙、糖2小匙、姜汁1小匙、香油1小匙。

【作法】
❶ 小黄瓜去头尾，洗净直剖成4等分，切段后置于大碗中。
❷ 红辣椒洗净切丝，加入❶内。
❸ 盐、糖、姜汁混匀后加入❶内，以筷子搅拌，置于冰箱冰凉后再倒入盘中，淋香油，撒芝麻即可食用。

Cold Dressed Cucumber

【Ingredients】
5 cucumbers, 1 red chilli, a dash of white sesame.

【Seasoning】
2 tbsp. of low soduim salt, 2 tbsp. of sugar, 2 tbsp. of ginger juice, 1 tbsp. of white sesame oil.

【Methods】
❶ Clean the cucumbers, cut the top and bottom, by pieces, and quarter each. Put them on the large bowl.
❷ Clean and shred the red chilli, add it in❶.
❸ Mix the spicies and add it in❶. stir by chopsticks, keep it in refrigerator until it cool down, and put them on the dish. Spread white sesame oil and sesame.

- -

凉拌海带丝

【材料】
海带丝·················200 克
红辣椒·····················1 根
嫩姜·······················5 片

【调味料】
低钠盐2小匙、酱油2小匙、香油2小匙。

【作法】
❶ 海带丝泡水洗净，红辣椒、嫩姜片洗净切丝。
❷ 海带丝在沸水中稍加煮烫后，捞出浸于冷开水中，沥去水分盛盘。加入红辣椒丝、姜丝拌匀。
❸ 盐、酱油、加入❷中拌匀后，置于冰箱中冰凉，食用前淋香油。

Cold Dressed Kelp Shredded

【Ingredients】
200g. shredded kelp, 1 red chilli, 5 ginger slices.

【Seasoning】
2 tbsp. of low sodium salt, 2 tbsp. of soy sauce, 2 tbsp. of white sesame oil.

【Methods】
❶ Soak and Clean shredded kelp, shred the red chilli and slice ginger.
❷ Blanch the shredded kelp in boiling water, then cool down in cold water, strain and put them on the dish. Stir with red shredded chilli and shredded ginger.
❸ Add salt, soy sauce in❷, cool down in the refrigerator. Spread white sesame oil before serving.

菠萝苦瓜鸡
Bitter Gourd Chicken with Pineapple

【材料】
①鸡半只。
②苦瓜1条、腌菠萝6片。

【调味料】
(A)料：酒2大匙、盐适量。

【作法】
❶ 鸡洗净、剁块，余烫去血水备用。苦瓜洗净去籽、切块。
❷ 汤锅内加水，放入鸡块、菠萝片、苦瓜及酒，大火煮开后，改小火煮至肉烂，加盐调味即可食和。

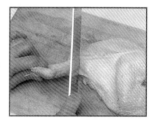

【Ingredients】
①½ free range chicken ②1 bitter gourd; 6 slices of salted pineapple.

【Seasoning】
(A) 2 tbsp. wine; proper salt

【Methods】
❶Rinse chicken, cut into pieces and blanch in boiling water. Rinse and remove the seeds of bitter gourd; cut into pieces.
❷put some water, chicken, pineapple, bitter gourd and wine in pot to cook with high heat. After boiling, turn to low heat to stew until chicken is soft. Add salt.

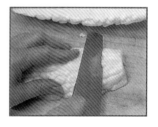

【功效】
清心明目，利尿消肿，美容、瘦身、祛热解毒。
【Efficiency】
Reduce a swelling and be diuretic; good for eyes. Detoxify.

蛤蜊冬瓜排骨汤
Wax Gourd Spareribs Soup with Clams

【材料】
① 蛤蜊 250 克。
② 冬瓜 500 克。
③ 排骨 600 克。
④ 嫩姜 1 块。

【调味料】
(A) 料：酒 1 茶匙、盐适量。

【作法】
❶ 蛤蜊泡盐水备用。冬瓜去皮切大块。排骨洗净，余烫去血水，嫩姜切丝。
❷ 锅内加水，先放入排骨，煮约 30 分钟后，再放入冬瓜和姜丝，至冬瓜熟软后，将蛤蜊放入，煮至蛤蜊开口，加(A) 料调味即可。

【Ingredients】
① 250g. clam ② 500g. wax gourd ③ 600g. spareribs ④ 1 baby ginger

【Seasoning】

(A) 1 tbsp. wine; proper salt

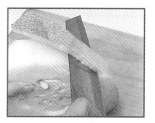

【Methods】
❶Soak clams in salty water. Pare wax gourd and then cut into pieces. Rinse and blanch spareribs in boiling water. Shred baby ginger.
❷Cook spareribs with water for about. 30 mins. and then put wax gourd and ginger. Add clams when wax gourd is soft. Add seasoning (A) when clams open.

【功效】
滋阴利水，可治喘、咳、痰多。
【Efficiency】
Cure asthma, coughing.

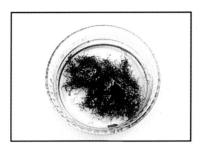

发菜金菇羹

【材料】

发菜……………………………………50 克
金针菇……………………………………1 大把
胡萝卜、竹笋……………………………各 1 小块
香菜………………………………………适量

【调味料】

低钠盐 2 小匙、乌醋 1 大匙、香油少许、素高汤 2
碗、淀粉、胡椒粉适量。

【作法】

❶ 发菜泡开洗净，金针菇氽烫、胡萝卜、竹笋切丝。
❷ 起油锅，将素高汤、❶ 的材料煮开后勾芡加调
   味料。
❸ 起锅前淋上香油、撒上香菜即可。

Golden Mushroom Thicken Soup with Hair Weeds

【Ingredients】

50g. hair weeds, 1 banch of golden mushroom, 1 cube
of carrot and bamboo shoot, parsley.

【Seasoning】

2 tbsp. of low sodium salt, 1 tbsp. black vinegar, white
sesame oil, 2 bowls of vegetarian broth, cornstarch,
pepper.

【Methods】

❶ Soak and rinse the hair weeds in water, clean and
   blanch the golden mushrooms, shredd the carrot,
   bamboo shoots.
❷ Heat oil, cook the ❶ingredients in broth and thicken,
   add spicies.
❸ Spread white sesame oil and parsley before turn off.

125

糙米粥
Unpolished Congee

【材料】
① 鸡腿 1 只。
② 糙米 1 杯、水 8 杯。
③ 胡萝卜 1 根、芹菜 1 棵。

【调味料】
(A) 料：盐、胡椒粉适量。

【作法】
❶ 鸡腿洗净，剁块，余烫去血水。糙米洗净，泡水约 4 小时。胡萝卜去皮、刨丝。芹菜去叶、切末。
❷ 先将糙米煮至半熟时，再放入鸡肉、胡萝卜丝同煮，小火煮约 40 分钟后，加 (A) 料调味，再撒上芹菜末即可。

【Ingredients】
① 1 chicken leg ② 1 cup of unpolished rice; 8 cups of water ③1 carrot; 1 celery

【Seasoning】
(A) proper salt and pepper powder

【Methods】
❶Rinse and cut chicken leg into pieces; then blanch in boiling water. Rinse unpolished rice and soak for 4 hours. Pare and shred carrot. Remove the leaves of celery and mince.
❷Cook unpolished rice; put chicken, carrot when rice turn to be medium done; turn to low heat to cook for 40 mins. Add seasoning (A) and sprinkle celery.

【功效】
健脾胃，强筋骨，增体力。

【Efficiency】
Good for spleen and stomach. Strengthen the body.

茯苓粥
Tuckahoe Congee

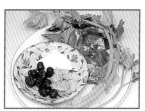

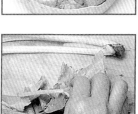

【材料】
① 小排骨 300 克。
② 茯苓、百合各 5 克、红枣 8 粒。
③ 米 1 杯、水 8 杯。
④ 芹菜 1 棵。

【调味料】
(A) 料：胡椒粉、盐各适量。

【作法】
❶ 小排骨洗净，余烫去血水。茯苓、百合、红枣泡水备用。芹菜去叶，洗净，切末。米洗净。
❷ 锅内加水，放入米，大火煮开后，改小火煮约 30 分钟，加入全部材料（除芹菜外），再煮约 30 分钟，加 (A) 料调味，再撒上芹菜末即可。

【Ingredients】
①300g. sparerib ②5g. each of tuckahoe and lily bulb. 8 red dates ③1 cup of rice; 8 cups of water ④ 1 celery.

【Seasoning】
(A) proper pepper powder and salt

【Methods】
❶Rinse spareribs and blanch in boiling water. So ak tuckahoe, lily bulb and red dates. Remove the leaves of celery, rinse and mince. Rinse rice.
❷Put water and rice in pot to cook with high heat; after boiling, turn to low heat to continue cooking for 30 mins. and put all ingredients except celery; cook for 30 mins more. Add seasoning (A) and sprinkle minced celery.

【功效】
滋阴清热，健脾祛湿，补虚益气。

【Efficiency】
Good for spleen. Cure rheumatism.

何首乌炖鳗鲡鱼
Stew Man Li-Fish with He Shou Wu

【材料】
①鳗鲡鱼1条。
②何首乌10克、当归2片、枸杞7.5克、山药10克、红枣8粒。
③老姜1块。

【调味料】
(A)料：米酒2大匙、盐适量。

【作法】
❶ 鳗鲡鱼去内脏，洗净切两段。药材快速冲洗后沥干备用。红枣泡软，老姜切片。
❷ 炖锅内加适量水，先将药材、姜片放入，煮开，改小火熬煮约30分钟，再将鱼放入煮熟，加(A)料调味后即可。

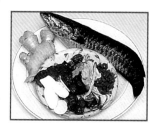

【Ingredients】
① 1 Man Li-Fish ② 10g. polygonum multiflorum (He Shou Wu); 2 slices of angelica, 7.5g. fruit of Chinese wolfberry, 10g. Chinese yam, 8 red dates. ③ 1 ginger

【Seasoning】
(A) 2 tbsp. rice wine; proper salt.

【Methods】
❶Remove viscera of Man Li-Fish and rinse; cut it into two parts. Rinse herbage; drain. Soak red dates. Slice ginger.
❷Cook herbage, ginger with water; after boiling, turn to low heat to stew for about. 30 mins. and then put Man Li-Fish to cook until it is soft, add seasoning (A).

【功效】
活血祛风，强健筋骨，美容养颜，可治筋骨酸痛，血虚遗精。
【Efficiency】
Strengthen the body; cure aching muscles and bones and nocturnal emission.

素肉羹

【材料】

素肉羹……………………………………1碗
香菇……………………………………3朵
竹笋……………………………………1支
胡萝卜…………………………………1/3根
香菜……………………………………少许

【调味料】

(A)料：低钠盐2小匙、糖1小匙、酱油1大匙、乌醋1大匙、胡椒少许。
(B)料：米酒少许、素高汤6杯。
(C)料：香油少许、淀粉3大匙。

【作法】

❶ 香菇、竹笋、胡萝卜均切丝。
❷ 放1大匙油，先将香菇丝爆香，再加素肉羹、竹笋、胡萝卜，淋上少许酒拌炒，注入高汤、(A)料煮约1分钟。
❸ 水淀粉勾芡。起锅前加入香油、胡椒粉、香菜即可享用。

Meatless Thicken Soup

【Ingredients】

1 bowl of meatless thicken, 3 black mushrooms, 1 bamboo shoot, 1/3 carrot, parsley.

【Seasoning】

(A) 2 tbsp. of low sodium salt, 1 tbsp. of sugar, 1 tbsp. of soy sauce, 1 tbsp. of black vinegar, pepper.
(B) Rice wine, 6 cups of vegetarian broth.
(C) White sesame oil, 3 tbsp. of cornstarch.

【Methods】

❶Shred black mushrooms, bamboo shoot, carrot.
❷Heat 1 tbsp. of oil, sante the black mushrooms, add meatless thicken, bamboo shoot, carrot, fry with wine, pour the broth, add (A) spicies for 1 minute.
❸Thicken by cornstarch. Sprinkle white sesame oil, pepper, parsley before serving.

木瓜花生炖猪蹄

Stew Pig's Hocks with Papaya and Peanuts

【材料】
①猪蹄 5 只
②花生 200 克。
③半熟木瓜 1 个。
④红枣 8 粒。

【调味料】
(A) 料：米酒 2 大匙、盐适量。

【作法】
❶ 猪蹄洗净，余烫去血水。花生洗净、泡水约 1 小时。木瓜去皮、去籽、切块。红枣泡软、去籽。
❷ 锅内加 10 杯水，放入猪蹄、花生及红枣，煮开后转小火炖煮约 1 小时，再将木瓜放入，加(A)料调味，续煮至猪蹄酥烂即可。

【Ingredients】
①5 pig's hocks ②200g. peanuts ③1 papaya ④8 red dates

【Seasoning】
(A) 2 tbsp. rice wine; proper salt.

【Methods】
❶Rinse and blanch pig's hocks. Rinse peanuts and soak for 1 hour. Pare and pit papaya, then cube. Soak and pit red dates.
❷Stew pig's hocks, peanuts, red dates with 10 cups of water; after boiling, turn to low heat to stew for 1 hour, and then add papaya and seasoning (A); continue cooking until hocks are soft and done.

【功效】
补中益气、养血通乳。

【Efficiency】
Nourish vitality; make blood and help breast development.

虫草小排汤
Chong-Cao Sparerib Soup

【材料】
① 小排骨 600 克。
② 冬虫夏草 15 克、枸杞 10 克、红枣
8 粒、老姜 1 块。

【调味料】
(A)料：米酒 2 大匙、盐适量。

【作法】
❶ 小排骨洗净，氽烫去血水。药材稍
冲洗，红枣泡软，老姜洗净、切片。
❷ 炖锅内加水，放入全部材料，大火
煮开后，改小火炖约 1 小时，加(A)
料调味即可。

【Ingredients】
① 600g. sparerib ② 15g. Chinese caterpillar fungus (Dong Chong Xia Cao);
10g. fruit of Chinese wolfberry; 8 red
dates; 1 ginger.

【Seasoning】
(A) 2 tbsp. rice wine; proper salt.

【Methods】
❶ Rinse spareribs and blanch in boiling water. Rinse herbage. Soak red
dates. Rinse and slice ginger.
❷ Put water and all the ingredients in
pot to cook with high heat. After
boiling, turn to low heat to stew for
1 hour. Add seasoning (A).

【功效】
补虚损、益精气，可
治阳痿早泄。

【Efficiency】
Nourish vitality. Cure
impotence.

芡实猪尾汤
Pig's Tail Soup with Fox Nut

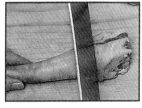

【材料】
① 猪尾 1 条。
② 芡实 200 克、莲子 150 克、薏仁 200
克。
③ 香菜 1 棵。

【调味料】
(A)米酒 2 大匙、盐适量。

【作法】
❶ 猪尾洗净、剁块、氽烫去血水。芡
实、薏仁泡水 30 分钟备用。香菜
洗净，切末。
❷ 锅内加水，将猪尾、芡实、薏仁放
入，大火煮开后转小火煮约 40 分
钟，再将莲子加入同煮，煮至猪尾
熟烂，加(A)料调味，再撒上香菜即
可。

【Ingredients】
① 1 pig's tail ② 200g. gorgon fruit;
150g. lotus seed; 200g. coix seed (Yi
Ren) ③ 1 coriander

【Seasoning】
(A) 2 tbsp. rice wine; proper salt

【Methods】
❶ Rinse and cut pig's tail into pieces.
Blanch in boiling water. Soak gorgon
fruit and Yi Ren for 30 mins. Rinse
and mince coriander.
❷ Put water, pig's tail, gorgon fruit and
Yi Ren in pot to cook with high heat;
after boiling, turn to low heat to cook
for 40 mins. add lotus seeds to cook
until pig's tail is soft and done. Add
seasoning (A). Sprinkle coriander.

【功效】
健脾止泻，补中益气，
固肾涩精。

【Efficiency】
Good for spleen and
kidney. Stop diarrhea.
Nourish vitality.

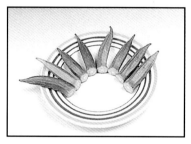

凉拌秋葵

Cold Dressed Okra

【材料】

秋葵……………………8 根

白芝麻………………2 大匙

【调味料】

酱油1小匙、素蚝油2大匙、糖少许、香油少许。

【作法】

❶ 秋葵去头洗净。

❷ 水煮沸，放1大匙盐、1小匙色拉油，秋葵放入煮约2分钟捞起放凉。

❸ 调味料拌匀，淋在秋葵上，再撒上白芝麻即可享用。

【Ingredients】

8 okras, 2 tbsp. of white sesame.

【Seasoning】

1 tbsp. of soy sauce, 2 tbsp. of vegetarian oyster sauce, sugar, white sesame oil.

【Methods】

❶ Cut the stem of okras and clean.

❷ Put 1 tbsp. of salt, 1 tbsp. of oil in boiling water, add okra to cook for 2 minutes, then drain and cool down.

❸ Stir spicies, sprinkle it over okras, then spread white sesame.

香酥腰果

Deep-Fried Cashew Nut

【材料】

腰果……………250 克

白芝麻………………适量

【调味料】

糖1½大匙、油3大匙。

【作法】

❶ 腰果洗净、沥干。

❷ 将腰果放入适量沸水中焖煮至熟，熄火后加糖拌匀，待凉。

❸ 锅内热3大匙油，以冷油方式倒入腰果炸成金黄色，撒上芝麻即可。

【Ingredients】

250g. cashew nuts, white sesame.

【Seasoning】

1½ tbsp. of sugar, 3 tbsp. of oil.

【Methods】

❶ Clean and drain the cashew nuts.

❷ Stew the cashew nuts in boiling water till it is well-done done. Turn the fire off and add sugar.

❸ Heat 3 tbsp. of oil, fry the cashew nuts to be golden, spread white sesames.

137

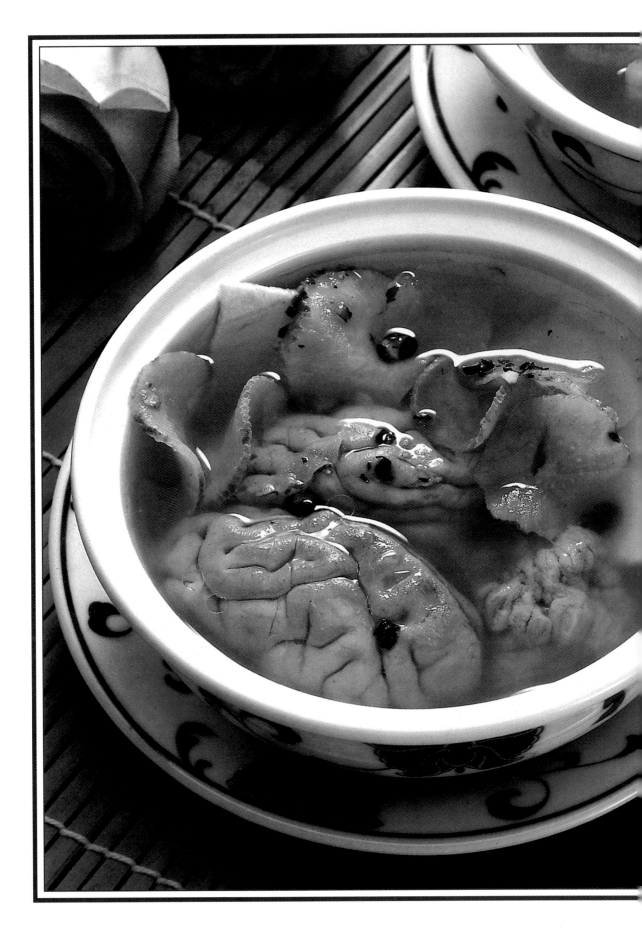

天麻安神汤
Stew Pig's Brain with Tian Ma

【材料】
①猪脑 1 副。
②天麻、茯苓各 10 克、酸枣仁 5 克。

【调味料】
(A) 料：米酒 2 大匙、盐 ½ 茶匙。

【作法】
❶ 猪脑洗净，用牙签挑去血丝及外膜，氽烫去腥。药材泡水备用。

❷ 炖锅内放入猪脑、药材、水及米酒，放入电锅内，外锅加半杯水，煮至开关跳起，加盐调味即可。

【Ingredients】
① 1 pair of pig's brain ② 10g. each of gastrodia elata (Tian Ma) and tuckahoe; 5g. spiny jujube seed (Suan Zao Ren)

【Seasoning】
(A) 2 tbsp. rice wine; ½ tsp. salt

【Methods】
❶ Rinse pig's brain, remove the membrane with a toothstick and then blanch it in boiling water. Soak all the herbage.

❷ Put pig's brain, herbage, water and rice wine in pot and then put the pot in the electric cooker; pour ½ cup of water outside the pot. Add salt after the switch turns off.

【功效】
养肝、宁神、补脑。
【Efficiency】
Good for liver and brain.

猪脊髓炖莲藕
Stew Pig's Spinal Cord with Lotus Root

【材料】
① 猪脊髓（连骨）600克。
② 莲藕3～4节、葱1根、姜1块。

【调味料】
(A) 料：米酒2大匙、盐适量。

【作法】
❶ 猪脊骨洗净、氽烫备用。莲藕去皮，切厚片。葱切段、姜切片。
❷ 备一炖锅，加水，将猪脊骨、莲藕、葱、姜片、米酒放入，煮开，再改小火煮约40分钟即可加盐调味食用。

【Ingredients】
① 600g. pig's spinal cord ② 3～4 nodes of lotus root; 1 scallion; 1 ginger

【Seasoning】
(A) 2 tbsp. rice wine; proper salt.

【Methods】
❶Rinse pig's spinal cord and blanch. Pare lotus root and cut into thick slices. Cut scallion into small sections. Slice ginger.
❷Put water, pig's spinal cord, lotus root, scallion, ginger and rice wine in pot to stew; after boiling, turn to low heat to cook for 40 mins.

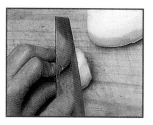

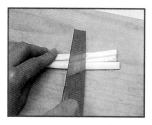

【功效】
补阴益髓。可治腰膝酸软，四肢无力。
【Efficiency】
Nourish vitality. Cure backache and weak limbs.

枸杞炖鳗

【材料】
素鳗……………………………200 克
红枣………………………………50 克
枸杞……………………………2 大匙
当归……………………………3 片
姜………………………………4 片

【调味料】
素高汤 6 杯、酒 2 大匙、香油 1 大匙。

【作法】
将所有材料放入炖锅，以大火蒸 25 分钟即可。

Steamed Eel with Wolfberry

【Ingredients】
200g. vegetarian eel, 50g. red jujube, 2 tbsp. of fruit of Chinese wolfberry, 3 pieces of angelica, 4 ginger slices.

【Seasoning】
6 cups of vegetarian broth, 2 tbsp. of wine 1 tbsp. of white sesame oil.

【Methods】
Put all ingredients in the stewing bowl, steam for 25 miniutes by high heat.

冬瓜鲤鱼汤
Carp Soup with Wax Gourd

【材料】
①鲤鱼1条。
②冬瓜1块，葱1根、嫩姜1块。

【调味料】
(A)料：酒1大匙、盐、香油适量。

【作法】
❶ 鲤鱼去内脏、鳞、洗净。冬瓜外皮冲洗干净，切片。葱切段。嫩姜切片。
❷ 锅内加水，放入所有材料，大火煮开后，改小火煮约40分钟，加(A)料调味即可。

【Ingredients】
① 1 carp ② 1 piece of wax gourd; 1 scallion; 1 baby ginger.

【Seasoning】
(A) 1 tbsp. wine, proper salt and sesame oil.

【Methods】
❶Remove the viscera and scale of carp and rinse. Rinse and slice wax gourd. Cut scallion into small sections. Slice ginger.
❷Put all the ingredients and water in pot to cook with high heat; after boiling, turn to low heat to cook for 40 mins. Add seasoning (A).

【功效】
清热解毒，利水消肿。

【Efficiency】
Relieve heat and neutralize poison. Reduce a swelling.

- -

参归猪肝汤
Pig's Liver Soup with Dang Shen and Angelica

【材料】
①猪肝250克。
②党参15克、当归3片、红枣8粒、姜1块、葱1根。

【调味料】
(A)料：酒1大匙、盐适量。

【作法】
❶ 猪肝洗净、切片。红枣泡软、姜切片、葱切段。
❷ 锅内加水，放入药材与姜片，大火煮开后，改小火煮约40分钟，开中火，放入猪肝、葱段，稍煮片刻，加(A)料调味即可。

【Ingredients】
①250g. pig's liver ②15g. codonopsis pilosula (Dang Shen); 3 slices of angelica root; 8 red dates; 1 ginger; 1 scallion

【Seasoning】
(A) 1 tbsp. wine; proper salt.

【Methods】
❶Rinse and slice pig's liver. soak red dates; slice ginger; cut scallion into small sections.
❷Cook herbage and ginger with water; after boiling, turn to low heat to cook for about. 40 mins. then turn to medium heat to cook for a while when put liver, scallion. Add seasoning (A).

【功效】
补血安神，可治失眠、血虚。

【Efficiency】
Make blood. Calm down the mind. Cure insomnia and weak body.

枸杞炖鳗
Stew River Eel with Wolfberry

【材料】
①鳗鱼1条。
②枸杞15克。
【调味料】
(A)料：米酒1杯。
【作法】
❶ 鳗鱼去内脏、洗净，切段。
❷ 炖锅内加水、酒、枸杞及鳗鱼，大火煮开后，改小火煮约40分钟，加盐调味即可。

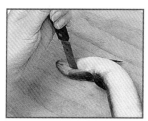

【Ingredients】
① 1 river eel ② 15g. fruit of Chinese wolfberry.
【Seasoning】
(A) 1 cup of rice wine.
【Methods】
❶Remove the riscera of river eel, rinse and cut it into small sections.
❷ Stew river eel with water, wine and fruit of Chinese wolfberry. After boiling, turn to low heat to cook for 40 mins. Add salt.

【功效】
明目、养颜、补精气。
【Efficiency】
Good for eyes and skin. Nourish vitality.

春饼

【材料】
春卷皮10张、豆芽250克、胡萝卜1/3根、豆腐干5片、小黄瓜2条、香菜少许。

【调味料】
低钠盐1大匙、香油少许、花生粉1碗、甜辣酱适量。

【作法】
❶ 豆芽去头，胡萝卜、豆腐干、小黄瓜均切丝。

❷ 豆芽、豆腐干、胡萝卜丝、小黄瓜丝分别入沸盐水中氽烫，捞起沥干后拌上香油。

❸ 春卷皮摊平，抹上一层甜辣酱，依序放入豆芽、豆腐干、胡萝卜、小黄瓜后撒些花生粉、香菜即可。

Spring Wrapper

【Ingredients】
10 pieces of spring wrapper, 250g. bean sprouts, 1/3 carrot, 5 pieces of dry bean curd, 2 cucumbers, parsley.

【Seasoning】
1 tbsp. of low sodium salt, white sesame, 1 bowl of peanut powder, sweet-spicy sauce.

【Methods】
❶ Cut the top of bean sprouts, shred carrot, dry bean curd, cucumbers.

❷ Blanch the bean sprouts, carrot, dry bean curd, cucumber in boiling salty water, drain and stir with white sesame oil.

❸ Daub the sweet-spicy sauce on the wrapper, put the bean sprouts, dry bean curds, carrot, cucumbers on, spread peanut powder, parsley, wrap it.

芝麻球

【材料】
糯米粉·····················3 杯
甜豆沙·····················1½ 杯
白芝麻·····················1 杯
【调味料】 水1杯、糖½杯。
【作法】
❶ 糖倒入水中完全溶化后，再加入糯米粉揉成光滑的长条面团，切成20小块，豆沙分成20份。

❷ 每块糯米包入1份豆沙揉成圆形，沾水后再滚上芝麻，并以轻搓糯米球的方式使芝麻固定。

❸ 将芝麻球入中温热油锅中炸成金黄色且胀大即可。

Deep-Fried Sesame Ball

【Ingredients】
3 cups of polished glutinous rice powder, 1½ cups of sweetened bean paste, 1 cup of white sesame.

【Seasoning】
1 cup of water, ½ cup of sugar.

【Methods】
❶ Put the sugar in water to melt, add glutinous rice powder, make it into strings (paste), cut into 20 pieces, also make the beanpaste into 20 pieces.

❷ Put each beanpaste into the glutinous rice wrapper, and make it into round ball. Spread a little of water and roll on sesame, fix the sesame on the ball.

❸ Fry the sesame balls to be golden by mid-heat

149

烧酒虾
Stew Prawns with Wine

【材料】
① 草虾 8 只。
② 当归 2 片、枸杞 10 克、黑枣 8 粒。 ③ 老姜 1 块。

【调味料】
(A)料：米酒 1 瓶。

【作法】
❶ 草虾去须足、剔去泥肠。枸杞、黑枣泡软。老姜切片。
❷ 将酒和全部材料放进锅内，煮开，点火将酒精燃烧后，再煮约 10 分钟即可。

【Ingredients】
① 8 prawns ② 2 slices of angelica; 10g. fruit of Chinese wolfberry; 8 black jujube ③ 1 ginger.

【Seasoning】
(A)1 bottle of rice wine.

【Methods】
❶Remove the palpus of prawns and de-vein. Soak fruit of Chinese wolfberry and black jujubes. Slice ginger.
❷Put wine and all the ingredients in pot to cook. After boiling, light a fire to burn the alcohol, and then cook for 10 mins. more.

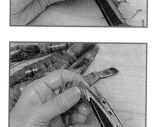

【功效】
补肾壮阳，可治肾虚阳痿。
【Efficiency】
Good for kidney. Cure impotence.

百合红枣莲子汤
Lotus Seed Soup with Lily Bulb and Red Dates

【材料】

① 百合 100 克、莲子 200 克、银耳 50
克、红枣 10 粒。

② 冰糖 4 大匙。

【作法】

❶ 百合、莲子洗净泡软。银耳泡软，
去蒂、分小朵。红枣泡软。

❷ 锅内放适量水，先放入莲子、红枣，
大火煮开后，改小火煮约 20 分钟，
再下百合、银耳续煮约 15 分钟，加
入冰糖即可。

【Ingredientsv】

① 100g. lily bulb; 200g. louts seed;
50g. tremella; 10 red dates; ② 4 tbsp.
rock candy

【Methods】

❶ Rinse and soak lily bulbs and lotus
seeds. Soak tremella and remove the
stems; divide them. Soak red dates.

❷ Put water, lotus seeds, red dates in
pot to cook with high heat; after
boiling, turn to low heat to cook for
20 mins. add lily bulbs and tremella;
keep cooking for 15 mins. more Add
rock candy.

【功效】

润肺止咳、益气、宁
神、清热润燥。

【Efficiency】

Moisten lung. Stop
coughing. Calm down
the mind.

红豆薏仁汤
Yi Ren Soup with Red Beans

【材料】

① 红小豆 250 克、红枣 20 粒、薏仁 250
克。

② 红砂糖适量。

【作法】

❶ 红小豆、薏仁洗净，泡水约 4 小时。
红枣泡软，去籽。

❷ 锅内加水，先放入红豆，大火煮开
后，转小火煮约 1 小时，再将薏仁、
红枣放入，煮至软烂，加入红砂糖
即可。

【Ingredients】

① 250g. small red bean; 20 red dates;
250g. coix seed (Yi Ren) ② proper red
granulated sugar

【Methods】

❶ Rinse red bean and Yi Ren; soak
them in water for 4 hours. Soak and
pit the red dates.

❷ Put water, red beans in pot to cook;
after boiling, turn to low heat to cook
for 1 hour; put Yi Ren and red dates
to continue cooking until they are
soft and done. Add red granulated
sugar.

【功效】

利水祛湿，可治水肿、
脚气病。

【Efficiency】

Cure rheumatism and
breiberi. Reduce
edema.

什锦沙拉

【材料】

苹果·······························1 个
胡萝卜·····························½ 根
小黄瓜·····························1 条
玉米粒·····························½ 杯
素火腿·····························⅓ 条
萝卜缨·····························1 小把
葡萄干·····························少许

【调味料】

糖 2 小匙、素沙拉酱 1 碗。

【作法】

❶ 苹果切丁、胡萝卜削皮洗净切丁煮熟，小黄瓜去头尾洗净切丁，素火腿切丁，与玉米粒同置大碗中。

❷ 将糖、沙拉酱调匀，和苹果丁、胡萝卜丁、小黄瓜丁、玉米粒、素火腿丁一同搅拌。

❸ 盘子以萝卜缨垫底，盛入什锦沙拉，洒上葡萄干即可。

Assorted Salad

【Ingredients】

1 apple, ½ carrot, 1 cucumber, ½ cup of corn, ⅓ vegetarian ham, a little of radish sprouts, raisins.

【Seasoning】

2 tbsp. of sugar, 1 bowl of salad dressing (vegetarian).

【Methods】

❶Strip the carrot off, dice the apple and the carrot, cook them well done. Dice the cucumber, vegetarian ham, put them on the bowl with corn.

❷Add the apple, carrot, cucumber, corn, vegetarian ham, stir with sugar and salad dressing.

❸Garnish the dish with radish sprouts, put the salad on, spread raisins.

冬瓜炖乌鱼
Stew Snakeheak Fish with Wax Gourd

【材料】
①乌鱼 1 条。
②冬瓜 500 克、红豆 150 克、姜 1 块。

【调味料】
(A) 料：米酒 2 大匙、盐、香油适量。

【作法】
❶ 乌鱼去内脏、洗净切两段备用。冬瓜（不去皮）洗净、切块、姜切片。红豆泡水 1 小时后，先煮约 40 分钟后捞出。

❷ 汤锅内加水，先放入红豆、姜片与冬瓜，煮约 20 分钟后将乌鱼与酒放入，煮至乌鱼、红豆熟烂后加盐、香油调味即可。

【Ingredients】
①1 snakehead fish ②500g. wax gourd; 150g. red bean; 1 ginger.

【Seasoning】
(A) 2 tbsp. rice wine, proper salt and sesame oil.

【Methods】
❶Remove the viscera of snakehead fish, rinse and cut into 2 sections. Rinse wax gourd, and cube. Slice ginger. Soak red beans for 1 hour and then cook for 40 mins.drain.

❷Stew red beans, ginger, wax gourd with water for 20 mins. then put snakehead fish and wine; continue cooking until fish and beans are soft and done. Add salt and sesame oil.

【功效】
补脾、利水、消肿。
【Efficiency】
Good for spleen. Reduce a swelling.

莲藕牛腩汤
Stew Chewy Beef with Lotus Root

【材料】
①牛腩600克。
②莲藕3～4节、葱1根、香菜1棵、姜1块、大蒜3粒、八角2粒。

【调味料】
(A) 料：酒2大匙、盐适量、酱油3大匙。

【作法】
❶ 牛腩洗净、切块、氽烫去血水。莲藕削去外皮，切成1公分厚片。葱切段、香菜切末、姜切片、大蒜拍碎。
❷ 备一深锅，将牛肉、莲藕、姜片、葱段、八角、大蒜、调味料(A)，全部放进，加水煮开后，转小火煮至肉烂即可。

【Ingredients】
①600g. chewy beef ②3～4 nodes of lotus root; 1 scallion; 1 coriander; 1 ginger, 3 garlic; 2 Japanese star anise

【Seasoning】
(A) 2 tbsp. rice wine; proper salt; 3 tbsp. soy sauce.

【Methods】
❶Rinse and cut chewy beef into small pieces. Blanch them in boiling water. Pare lotus root and cut into 1 cm-thick slices. Cut scallion into small sections. Mince coriander. Slice ginger. Chop garlic.
❷Stew chewy beef, lotus root, ginger, scallion, anise, garlic, seasoning (A) with water. After boiling, turn to low heat to cook until chewy beef is soft and done.

【功效】
清热凉血、消肿利水、强筋骨。
【Efficiency】
Relieve heat, reduce a swelling and strength the body.

海苔卷

【材料】
海苔·····················2 大张
绿芦笋·················2 根
素火腿·················2 片
胡萝卜···············1/2 根
（直切）
紫甘蓝·················1/5 个
【调味料】
素沙拉酱 1 碗。
【作法】
❶ 绿芦笋以水煮过，素火腿切条，胡萝卜去皮切长条烫煮，紫甘蓝切丝。
❷ 摊开海苔，放入绿芦笋 1 根，素火腿条，胡萝卜条，紫甘蓝，抹些沙拉酱后卷起，切小段即可食用。

Laver Wrapper

【Ingredients】
2 pieces of laver, 2 green asparagus, 2 slices of vegetarian ham, 1/2 carrot, 1/5 purple cabbage.
【Seasoning】
1 bowl of salad dressing (vegetarian).
【Methods】
❶ Strip the vegetarian ham, carrot, cook the green asparagus and carrot in water, shred purple cabbage.
❷ Put the green asparagus, vegetarian ham, carrot, purple cabbage on the laver, Paint the salad dressing on, wrap and cut it by pieces.

三色卷

【材料】
土司·····················4 片
素火腿·················4 片
西洋芹·················适量
【调味料】
沙拉酱 1 小碗。
【作法】
❶ 土司去硬边对切，素火腿对切，西洋芹泡冰水后沥去水分，切成与土司同宽的小段。
❷ 在土司上抹一层沙拉酱，放入素火腿和西洋芹段后卷起即可。

Triple Color Wrapper

【Ingredients】
4 pieces of toast, 4 slices of vegetarian ham, celery.
【Seasoning】
1 bowl of salad dressing.
【Methods】
❶ Cut the edge of toast off, and cut the vegetarian ham by cross, keep the celery in ice water, then cut as the same size as toast.
❷ Paint the dressing on the toast, put the vegetarian ham, celery and wrap it.

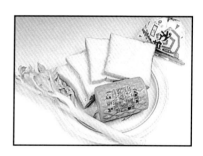

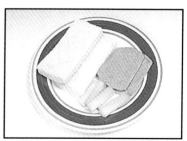

黄芪羊肉汤
Mutton Soup with Huang Qi

【材料】
① 羊肉 500 克。
② 黄芪 25 克、山药 20 克、枸杞 10 克、桂圆肉 10 克。
③ 老姜 1 块。

【调味料】
(A)料：盐适量。

【作法】
❶ 羊肉洗净，切块，汆烫去腥。药材稍冲洗，沥干备用。老姜切片。
❷ 炖锅内加水，将羊肉与药材、姜片等放入，大火烧开后改小火炖约 2 小时加(A)料调味即可。

【Ingredients】
① 500g. mutton ② 25g. astragalus membranaceus (Huang Qi); 20g. yam, 10g. wolfberry, 10g. dried longan ③ 1 ginger

【Seasoning】
(A)proper salt.

【Methods】
❶Rinse mutton; cut it into pieces and then blanch in boiling water. Rinse herbage and drain. slice ginger.
❶Put water, mutton, herbage and sliced ginger in pot to cook with high heat; after boiling, turn to low heat to stew for 2 hrs. Add seasoning (A).

【功效】
健脾补虚，增强体力。
【Efficiency】
Good for spleen. Nourish vitality.

牛膝杜仲汤
Niu Xi and Du Zhong Soup

【材料】
① 乌骨鸡半只。
② 牛膝 15 克、杜仲 25 克、红枣 8 粒。
③ 老姜 1 块、黑豆 150 克。

【调味料】
(A)料：酒 2 大匙、盐适量。

【作法】
❶ 乌骨鸡去油脂，洗净、剁块，汆烫去血水。药材稍冲洗，沥干。红枣泡软。老姜切片。黑豆泡软。
❷ 炖锅内加水，先放入药材，姜片与黑豆，大火煮开后炖约 30 分钟，将鸡肉放入，煮约 50 分钟，加(A)料调味即可。

【Ingredients】
① ½ dark-skinned chicken ② 15g. achy ranthes bidentata. (Niu Xi), 25g. eucommia bark (Du Zhong); 8 red dates. ③ 1 ginger; 150g. black soya bean (Hei Dou)

【Seasoning】
(A) 2 tbsp. wine; proper salt.

【Methods】
❶Clean and rinse chicken. Cut it into pieces and blanch in boiling water. Rinse herbage; drain. Soak red dates. Slice ginger. Soak Hei Dou.
❷Put water, herbage, ginger and Hei Dou in pot to cook with high heat; after boiling, continue cooking for about. 30 mins. and put chicken to cook for about. 50 mins. Add seasoning (A).

【功效】
祛瘀活血，强健筋骨。
【Efficiency】
Strengthen body. Improve blood circulation.

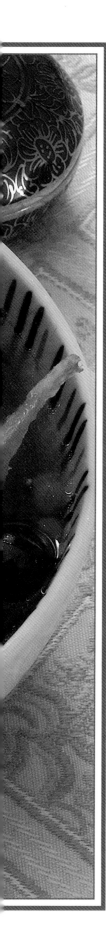

烧酒鸡
Stew Chicken with Wine

【材料】
① 鸡 1 只
② 市售烧酒鸡药材 1 包。
③ 米酒 3 瓶。

【作法】
❶ 鸡洗净，剁块，余烫去血水。药材快速冲洗，沥干水份备用。
❷ 取一深锅，放入鸡块与药材，再将米酒全部倒入，大火煮开后点火将酒精燃烧后，改小火煮至肉烂即可。

【Ingredients】
① 1 free range chicken ② 1 pkt. of mixed herbs ③ 3 bottles of rice wine.

【Methods】
❶Rinse chicken, cut into pieces and blanch in boiling water. Rinse herbage and drain.
❷Put chicken, herbage, rice wine in pot, then cook with high heat, ligh fire to burn out alcohol; then turn to low heat to stew until chicken is soft and done.

【功效】
血虚、冬天手脚冰冷者深具效用。
【Efficiency】
Improve hands and feet not to become cold during winter and nourish vitality.

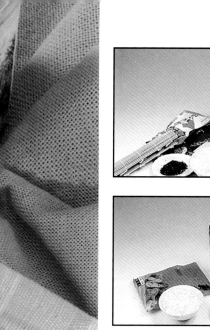

圆形寿司

【材料】

寿司饭⋯⋯⋯⋯⋯2碗　素火腿⋯⋯⋯⋯⋯1条
海苔⋯⋯⋯⋯⋯2大张　黑芝麻⋯⋯⋯⋯2大匙
小黄瓜⋯⋯⋯⋯⋯1条　竹帘⋯⋯⋯⋯⋯⋯1张
市售现成黄瓜丝⋯2条

【调味料】白醋 ½ 杯。

【作法】

❶ 将白醋、黑芝麻倒入热饭中拌匀。

❷ 小黄瓜以盐搓洗后去瓜瓤切长条，素火腿切长条。

❸ 海苔置于竹帘上摊平，将寿司饭铺满海苔 ²/₃ 面积，小黄瓜条、火腿条、黄瓜丝分别排于其上，用竹帘卷成长条，切段后即可食用。

Round Sushi

【Ingredients】

2 bowls of sushi rice, 2 pieces of laver, 1 cucumber, shredded cucumber, 1 vegetarian ham, 2 tbsp. of black sesame, 1 bamboo screen.

【Seasoning】 ½ cup of vinegar.

【Methods】

❶Stir the vinegar and black sesame with the hot rice.

❷Clean the cucumber by salty water, strip the cucumber and vegetarian ham.

❸Put the laver on the bamboo screen, add the sushi rice around the ²/₃ laver, put the cucumber, vegetarian ham, shredded cucumber orderly, wrap and cut by sections.

稻荷寿司

【材料】

寿司饭⋯⋯⋯⋯⋯2碗　黑芝麻⋯⋯⋯⋯3大匙
油豆腐皮1包（市售）　黑豆（市售，已煮软）适量

【调味料】白醋 ½ 杯。

【作法】

❶ 将白醋、黑芝麻倒入热饭中拌匀。

❷ 打开油豆腐皮，从袋口 ¼ 处往内摺，再装入寿司饭，饭上放黑豆即可。

Waterlily Sushi

【Ingredients】

2 bowls of sushi rice, 1 pack of oiled dried bean curd, 3 tbsp. of black sesame, black beans (soft, well-done).

【Seasonig】½ cup of vinegar.

【Methods】

❶Stir the vinegar, black sesame with the hot rice.

❷Open the oiled dried bean curd, fold it inside form the ¼ edge, put the rice inside, add black beans on rice.

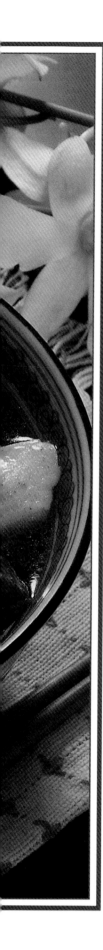

鲍鱼杜仲炖老鸭
Stew Duck with Abalone and Du Zhong

【材料】
①鸭半只。
②鲍鱼1只。
③杜仲15克、枸杞10克。老姜1块。

【调味料】
(A)料：酒2大匙、盐适量。

【作法】
❶ 鸭去杂质、洗净，剁块，氽烫去血水。鲍鱼切片。药材稍冲洗，老姜切片。

❷ 炖锅加水，放入全部材料，煮开后转小火，熬煮约2小时至肉烂，加(A)料调味即成。

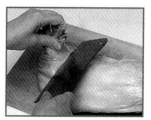

【Ingredients】
①½ mature duck ②1 abalone ③15g. eucommia bark (Du Zhong); 10g. wolfberry; 1 ginger

【Seasoning】
(A) 2 tbsp. wine; proper salt.

【Methods】
❶Clean and rinse duck; cut it into small pieces and then blanch in boiling water. Slice abalone. Rinse herbage and slice ginger.

❷Put some water, all the ingredients in pot to cook with high heat; after boiling, turn to low heat to stew for about 2 hours until duck is soft and done. Add seasoning (A).

【功效】
滋肝补肾，强筋健骨，可治产后体虚，腰膝酸痛。
【Efficiency】
Good for liver and kidney. Strengthen the body. Cure weak body after childbirth and backache.

桂圆粥
Dry Longan Congee

【材料】
① 圆糯米半杯。
② 桂圆肉 100 克。
③ 红砂糖 3 大匙。

【作法】
❶ 圆糯米洗净，泡水 2 小时。
❷ 圆糯米加水 4 杯，煮约 30 分钟后，加入桂圆肉与红砂糖，再熬煮 10 分钟即可。

【Ingredients】
① ½ Polished glutinous rice ② 100g. dried longan ③ 3 tbsp. Red granulated sugar

【Methods】
❶ Rinse rice and soak in water for 2 hours.
❷ Cook rice with 4 cups of water for 30 mins. add dried longan and red granulated sugar; stew for 10 mins. more.

【功效】
开胃健脾，增强体力，养血安神。

【Efficiency】
Good for spleen and kidney. Strengthen the body. Nourish vitality. Calm down the mind.

芡实莲子薏仁汤
Yi Ren Soup with Gorgon Fruit and Lotus Seeds

【材料】
① 芡实 150 克、莲子 100 克、薏仁 150 克、红枣 6 粒。
② 冰糖 5 大匙。

【作法】
❶ 芡实、莲子、薏仁洗净，泡水约 30 分钟。红枣洗净泡软。
❷ 炖锅内加水，先将芡实、薏仁放进，大火煮开后，转小火煮约 30 分钟后，再将莲子、红枣放入，续煮约 30 分钟，加入冰糖即可。

【Ingredients】
① 150g. gorgon fruit; 100g. lotus seeds; 150g. coix seeds (Yi Ren); 6 red dates
② 5 tbsp. rock candy

【Methods】
❶ Rinse gorgon fruit, lotus seeds and Yi Ren; soak them in water for 30 mins. Rinse and soak red dates.
❷ Put water, gorgon fruit, Yi Ren in pot to cook with high heat; after boiling, turn to low heat to continue cooking; 30 mins. later, put lotus seeds and red dates and keep cooking for 30 mins. Add rock candy.

【功效】
生津滋养、益血气。健脾、宁神。利水消肿、美白肌肤。

【Efficiency】
Help blood circulation. Calm down the mind. Reduce a swelling. Good for spleen and skin.

寿桃

【材料】

中筋面粉……………2 杯
甜豆沙………………1 杯
发酵粉………………1 小匙
食用红色素…………少许

【调味料】

油 ½ 大匙、水 ½ 杯、低钠盐 1 小匙。

【作法】

❶ 发酵粉加入面粉及调味料，揉成面团，切成 10 等份，豆沙亦分成 10 等份。

❷ 每份面团擀成中间厚、边缘薄的面皮，包入豆沙后收口捏合成桃状，置于纸上发酵半小时，以大火蒸 15 分钟。

❸ 以牙刷沾食用红色素水后，利用汤匙弹动牙刷上色即可。

Chinese Birthday Cake

【Ingredients】

2 cups of flour, 1 cup of sweet sweetened bean paste, 1 tbsp. of soda powder, edible red pigment.

【Seasoning】

½ tbsp. of oil, ½ cup of water, 1 tbsp. of low sodium salt.

【Methods】

❶ Stir soda powder, flour, spicies to become paste, cut it into 10 sections, also divide the beanpaste into 10 parts.

❷ Stretch each paste with the middle thick, the edge thin, put the beanpaste on, make it like a peach, put them on the paper to ferment for half an hour, stew for 15 minutes by high heat.

❸ Put the edible red pigment on the tooth brush, knock the tooth brush by a spoon to color it.

素饺

【材料】

水饺皮 500 克、圆白菜 ¼ 个、胡萝卜 ⅓ 根、香菇 4 朵、五香豆腐干 4 片、姜 1 片、粉丝 1 小包。

【调味料】

低钠盐 1 大匙、胡椒少许、香油少许。

【作法】

❶ 粉丝泡软后切碎，胡萝卜、香菇、豆腐干、姜均切细末，圆白菜切碎。

❷ 锅内放少许油炒胡萝卜、香菇、豆腐干，圆白菜以少许盐腌 50 分钟后挤干水分。

❸ 将粉丝、❷的材料连同调味料、姜末一起拌匀包成饺子，入蒸笼大火蒸 5 至 7 分钟即可。

Vegetarian Dumpling

【Ingredients】

500g. dumpling wrapper, ¼ cabbage, ⅓ carrot, 4 black mushrooms, 4 pieces of five spicies dry bean curd, 1 sliced ginger, 1 pack of bean vermicelli.

【Seasoning】

1 tbsp. of low sodium salt, pepper, white sesame oil.

【Methods】

❶ Soak the bean vermicelli and chop. Chop the carrot, black mushrooms, dry bean curds, ginger and cabbage.

❷ Fry the carrot, black mushrooms, dry bean curd and cabbage. Pickle with salt for 50 mins. Then drain up.

❸ Stir the bean vermicelli and ❷ ingredients, spicies, ginger chopped. Make them into dumplings. steam for 5-7 minutes by high heat.

糙米鸡

Stew Chicken with Unpolished Rice Soup

【材料】
①鸡半只。
②糙米 1½ 杯。
③香菜 2 棵。
④红枣 10 粒.

【调味料】
(A) 料：米酒 2 大匙、盐、胡椒粉适量。

【作法】
❶ 糙米洗净，泡水约 2 小时后，加水 10 杯，熬煮约 1 小时后，将米汤沥出。香菜洗净切末，红枣泡软备用。
❷ 鸡去油脂、洗净，剁块，汆烫备用。
❸ 取一炖锅，将糙米汤加入，接着放入鸡肉与红枣，炖煮至肉烂，加调味料(A)调味即可，食用时加上香菜则更加美味。

【Ingredients】
① ½ free range chicken ② 1½ cup of unpolished rice ③ 2 coriander ④ 10 red dates

【Seasoning】
(A) 2 tbsp. rice wine; proper pepper powder

【Methods】

❶Rinse unpolished rice and then soak for 2 hours. Cook rice with 10 cups of water for 1 hour and then remove the rice out. Rinse and mince coriander. Soak red dates.
❷Rinse and cut chicken into small pieces; blanch in boiling water.
❸Put the rice soup in a pot, and then add chicken, red dates, to stew until chicken is soft and done. Add seasoning (A). Sprinkle cordiander before eating.

【功效】
滋阴补气，养脾健胃。
【Efficiency】
Nourish vitality. Good for spleen and stomach.

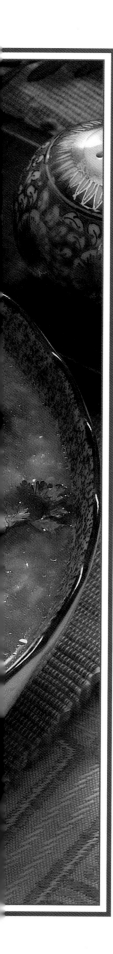

枸杞鲈鱼汤
Stew Sea Bass with Wolfberry

【材料】
① 鲈鱼 1 条。
② 当归 2 片、枸杞 10 克。
③ 嫩姜 1 块、紫苏少许。

【调味料】
(A) 料：酒 1 大匙、盐适量。

【作法】
❶ 鲈鱼去鳞、鳃、内脏后，洗净，切两段。药材快速冲洗沥干水份。嫩姜切丝，紫苏洗净。

❷ 锅内加水，先将药材煮开后转小火熬煮约5分钟后，将鱼和姜丝放入，煮熟，加(A) 料调味后即可，食用时加入紫苏，则更加美味。

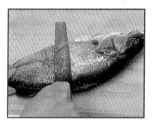

【Ingredients】
① 1 sea bass ② 2 slices of angelica; 10g. fruit of Chinese wolfberry ③ 1 baby ginger; a dash of basil

【Seasoning】
(A) 1 tbsp. wine; proper salt

【Methods】
❶ Remove the scale, gill and viscera of sea bass, then rinse and cut into two sections. Rinse herbage and drain. Shred ginger. Rinse basil.

❷ Cook herbage with water; after boiling, turn to low heat to cook for 5 mins. more put sea bass and ginger to continue cooking, add seasoning (A). Add basil before eating, the taste will be better.

【功效】
健脾利水，益肾安胎，能促进伤口愈合。

【Efficiency】
Good for spleen and kidney. Cure wound.

素包子

Vegetarian Stuffed Bun

【材料】
中筋面粉3杯、发酵粉1小匙、圆白菜¼个、香菇3朵、豆腐干3片、竹笋½个、姜1片。

【Ingredients】
3 cups of flour, 1 tbsp. of soda powder, ¼ cabbage, 3 black mushrooms, 3 pieces of dry bean curd, ½ bamboo shoot, 1 slice of ginger.

【调味料】
水1杯、低钠盐2小匙、香油少许、胡椒少许。

【Seasoning】
1 cup of water, 2 tbsp. of low sodium salt, white sesame oil, pepper.

【作法】
❶ 面粉加½小匙盐和1小匙发酵粉揉成面团，擀成中厚边薄的面皮。

❷ 圆白菜切碎，香菇泡软去蒂，竹笋剥皮洗净，与豆腐干一起切细丁，姜切末。

❸ 圆白菜与少许盐腌50分钟后挤干水分，锅内放少许油爆香香菇，再加竹笋、豆腐干同炒。

❹ 将 ❸ 的材料连同1½小匙盐、香油、胡椒、姜末一起拌匀包成包子，入蒸笼以大火蒸10至15分钟。

【Methods】
❶ Stir the flour, ½ tbsp. of salt, 1 tbsp. of soda powder into paste, stretch each into wrapper.

❷ Chop the cabbage, soak the black mushrooms and cut the stems off. Strip and clean bamboo shoot. Dice the dry bean curds and bamboo shoot. Chop ginger.

❸ Pickle the cabbage with a little of salt for 50 minutes and drain. Sante the black mushrooms, fry bamboo shoots and dry bean curds.

❹ Stir ❸ ingredients with 1½ tbsp. of salt, white sesame oil, pepper, ginger chopped, make it into stuffed bun. Steam for 10～15 minutes by high heat.

豆沙包

Mashed Bean Stuffed Bun

【材料】
中筋面粉·················2 杯
甜豆沙·················1 杯
发酵粉·················1 小匙

【Ingredients】
2 cups of flour, 1 cup of mashed beans, 1 tbsp. of soda powder.

【调味料】
水½杯、低钠盐1小匙。

【Seasoning】
½ cup of water, 1 tbsp. of low sodium salt.

【作法】
❶ 发酵粉加入面粉及调味料，揉成面团，切成10等份，发酵约30分钟，豆沙亦分成10等份。

❷ 每份面团擀成中间厚，边缘薄的面皮，包入豆沙后收口捏合，置于蒸笼内，以大火蒸15分钟。

【Methods】
❶ Stir the soda powder, flour and spicies into wrapper, cut it into 10 sections. ferment for 30 minutes. Also cut mashed bean into 10 parts.

❷ Stretch the wrapper with the middle thick, the edge thin, put the mashed bean in, and close. Steam for 15 minutes by high heat.

玉竹沙参炖老鸭
Stew Duck with Yu Zhu and Sha Shen

【材料】
① 老鸭1只。
② 玉竹、沙参各40克、枸杞10克。

【作法】
❶ 鸭去杂质，洗净，剁块，氽烫去腥。药材稍冲洗。
❷ 备一深锅，将药材、鸭肉放入，加水煮开后，改小火
　 炖煮至肉烂即可。

【Ingredients】
① 1 mature duck ② 40g. each of fragrant solomonseal rhizome (Yu Zhu) and root of straight ladybell (Sha Shen); 10g. medlar.

【Methods】
❶Clean and rinse duck; cut it into pieces and then blanch in boiling water. Rinse herbage.
❷Put herbage, duck and water in pot to cook until boiling; turn to low heat to stew until duck is soft and done.

【功效】
清肺祛燥、止咳消炎。
【Efficiency】
Good for lung. Stop coughing. Eliminate inflammation.

图书在版编目(CIP)数据

养生食补/黄怀玲 林淑莲著.
北京：外文出版社，2002.6
(中华美食系列)

ISBN 7-119-03083-3

Ⅰ.养… Ⅱ.①黄… ②林… Ⅲ.保健 - 食谱 Ⅳ.TS972.161

中国版本图书馆 CIP 数据核字 (2002) 第 036781 号

外文出版社网址：
 http://www.flp.com.cn
外文出版社电子信箱：
 info@flp.com.cn
 sales@flp.com.cn

著作权合同登记图字：2002-1351
中文简体字版权由台湾华文网股份有限公司授权

中华美食系列(3)
养生食补

著　　者　黄怀玲 林淑莲
责任编辑　刘慧
印刷监制　韩少乙
出版发行　外文出版社
社　　址　北京市百万庄大街24号　　　　邮政编码　100037
电　　话　(010)68320579(总编室)
　　　　　(010)68329514 / 68327211(推广发行部)
制　　作　外文出版社照排中心
印　　刷　北京外文印刷厂
经　　销　新华书店／外文书店
开　　本　16开(787 × 1092毫米)　　　字　数　30千字
印　　数　0001-3000册　　　　　　　　印　张　11.50
版　　次　2002年第1版第1次印刷
装　　别　平
书　　号　ISBN 7-119-03083-3/J · 1604(外)
定　　价　80.00元